THE
SINGLE
MOTHER'S
HANDBOOK

THE SINGLE MOTHER'S HANDBOOK

BY ELIZABETH S. GREYWOLF

Quill

New York   1984

Library of Congress Catalog Card Number: 83-62356

ISBN 0-688-02260-X
ISBN 0-688-02261-8 (pbk.)

Printed in the United States of America

First Quill Edition

1 2 3 4 5 6 7 8 9 10

BOOK DESIGN BY PATTY LOWY

Foreword

A few years ago the word *stress* probably conjured up for most of us images of brain surgeons, Arctic explorers, or high-powered executives: people (mostly men) in exotic and prestigious professions. Today we recognize that some of the most stressful and demanding occupations are neither exotic nor particularly prestigious, and they are certainly not confined to men. We know now that the day-in, day-out demands of parenting requires tremendous stores of energy and resilience. Taking care of children, ensuring their health and safety, and providing for their emotional needs turn out to be tasks that are as stressful as they are important.

Stress levels can rise especially high when there is no other adult who shares in the demands of parenting or when economic problems complicate the tasks of raising a family. The single mother may find she is constantly needed by others, constantly giving to others, always in a hurry. She may find that she is always looking after other people and forgetting to look after herself.

Foreword

While solo parenting is challenging and demanding, it can also bring tremendous satisfactions. The single mother can protect herself from the ravages of stress while enjoying herself and her children to the full. What it takes are the sort of "discoveries" that Elizabeth Greywolf has made, and has shared in this remarkable book. While there are no magic formulas here to add extra hours to the day or to make all the bills disappear, there are powerful ideas to help make the most of each hour and to put economic arrangements on a sounder footing. Most important of all, there is much wisdom here on taking care of oneself and understanding how to keep stress from taking a physical or emotional toll. While so many demands in a single mother's life are important, if she loses sight of her own needs in attending to those of others, the center will not hold. Understanding and responding to one's own needs can provide the health and vigor that make it possible to fulfill other responsibilities and that keep those responsibilities in perspective.

This book grew out of a research project in which women shared their experiences and ideas for the purpose of greater understanding. It was the hope of everyone involved that the understanding that was achieved could be useful to other women. Elizabeth Greywolf has made that hope a reality. She has gone beyond one specific study to consider the whole woman—body and soul—who is engaged in the demanding role of single parent. This book should help many, many women make that demanding role a rewarding one as well.

—DEBORAH BELLE, Ed.D.
Director, Stress and
Families Project
Harvard University, 1977–1982
Assistant Professor of Psychology,
Boston University

Contents

Contents

INTRODUCTION

Becoming a single mother is such a major transition that it automatically triggers a multitude of changes. Some of these changes are as dramatic as events that occur to families during times of war: loss of a life partner and economic provider; and a restructuring of old habits and ways of looking at the world which may include changing homes and old friends. Some of the changes single parenting brings are much less dramatic. But they may be as wearing, on a day-to-day basis, as drops of water on stone.

Perhaps you have become a single mother through an unexpected pregnancy, or through the death of your husband. More likely, you have gone through a divorce or separation. However you have arrived at this point in your life, you need to know how to cope successfully with all the resulting changes. You need to know how to secure life's basics, and how to pass them on to your children with a minimum of stress and a maximum of laughter.

If you have limited life experiences and/or limited resources, single-parenting responsibilities can feel overwhelming. Even for women who have extensive experiences in the world, the going can, occasionally, be very difficult. Simply having to juggle the double duties of a mother and a father can, from time to time, shoot your stress level sky high.

In the United States, one child in five (12.5 million) now lives in a single-parent household. The single-parent home is the fastest growing alternative to the traditional nuclear family. As this trend continues, it becomes more and more important for society to know what can provide a buffer to the stresses that play havoc with the single mother's mental and physical health. For when mothers aren't as healthy as they can be, their children suffer also.

America is currently far behind many European countries in providing the kinds of options that make single parenting an easier task. There are relatively few reasonably priced day-care centers. And private industries are slow to offer alternative work arrangements—such as flextime jobs, split shifts, and on-site nurseries for working mothers. Until these and other changes are made on a large scale within society, single parents are left to cope with their double-duty jobs in the best ways they can.

Most women are still awarded custody of their children after separation. Usually they wind up with the responsibilities that the fathers of their children do not meet. Most end up responsible for full or major financial support of their families, since child-support payments are often unrealistically low or nonexistent. An increasing number of single mothers are, therefore, working at full-time jobs—as providers and homemakers. These are the Supermoms, women who are putting in an eighty-hour-plus week and who are often stressed to the limit in doing so.

Millions of women, however, are unable to find work that can support their families. These women turn to welfare as a last resort. What they find is not the free ride that welfare may appear to be. Mothers on welfare face not only the stigma of having hit bottom but also the constant struggle to make ends meet on poverty-level budgets.

How are single mothers coping with their two-parent responsibilities? Increasingly women are talking to each other about just how it's done, what makes single parenting easier, and what makes it especially difficult. Now, as well as ideas, women are sharing their time and energy. And they are beginning to act as a bloc to bring about changes that make their lives happier and more satisfying. A growing number of single mothers are joining together in local communities everywhere, channeling their resources into preschool nurseries and play groups, babysitting and car pools, professional work groups, consciousness-raising sessions, and social groups to ease their transition into the community as singles.

The average single mother's life is vastly improved by connections with supportive and knowledgeable people in her community. But the ultimate task of single parenting—securing a better tomorrow for herself and her children—falls primarily on the single mother's shoulders. If those shoulders are as strong as they can be, the job is an easier and more gratifying one.

The data on which this book is based were gathered from hundreds of women who are carrying a great deal of the burden of their families. I am very grateful for their willingness to share what they have learned as mothers and as women in transition. My hope is that out of that sharing will come more positive and energizing discoveries for single mothers everywhere.

CHAPTER ONE

The Fine Art of Juggling

Once there was a juggler who worked in a circus. This juggler had practiced very hard to get to be as good as she possibly could be. For a long time she'd worked at perfecting her skills, managing to keep six green and blue balls in the air, along with assorted vegetables and two flaming sticks. It took a lot of skill and concentration, but the juggler managed to do her act very well, three times a night in the Big Top Circus.

Then one morning her boss, the Ringmaster, called the juggler in for a talk. The Ringmaster said he wanted the juggler to add a watermelon, three more flaming sticks, and a live puppy to the things already being juggled. And that he wanted her to perform five times a night instead of three. And the Ringmaster wanted her to start doing that tomorrow!

We don't know whether or not the juggler in the story was ever able to balance all the things the Ringmaster wanted her to. But any single mother would find it very easy to imagine just how the juggler felt when she heard what new things were expected of her. Trying to balance the hassles of work and child care, of money, meals, and discipline on top of daily house-keeping can feel an awful lot like being in the juggler's shoes.

THE PROFESSION WITHOUT PAY

Of the thousands of different jobs available—everything from astronaut to zoo keeper—some are more fun than others. And some are especially noted for causing high levels of tension in the people who do them.

For instance, it has become widely accepted that many professional jobs with heavy responsibilities (like doctoring) also come with very high levels of stress. But what a lot of people haven't realized until recently is that most single parents (especially women) are living with day-to-day stresses that are, like some doctors', far above normal.

Few single mothers would find this surprising. If you have been solo parenting for a while, you know how hard your job is. A single parent needs an abundance of patience. Like a doctor, in addition to your twenty-four-hour-a-day on-call responsibilities, you probably have few relaxing weekends as well as too frequent emergency situations. You must also wade through conflicting masses of health information in an effort to ward off physical sickness and to keep your family emotionally stable.

On top of all this, mothers are expected to be efficiency experts, chauffeurs, accountants, safety experts, teacher's aides, and child psychologists. No paid profession requires so many diverse talents and skills. And all this is done by single mothers who manage financial support as well!

How do women do all this? What do they find most difficult about this incredible juggling act? And what have they learned that can help other women juggle all the stresses of solo parenting more easily?

To find out the answers to these and other questions, the Stress and Families Project was organized at Harvard University under a grant from the Mental Health Services branch of the National Institutes of Mental Health. A four-year research-into-action project, Stress and Families involved hundreds of people and became one of the most comprehensive projects of its kind. Two studies were recently completed, involving more than 240 women now living in the Boston area, although many have lived in other parts of the country and should reflect experiences shared by women across the nation.

WHY DO I FEEL THIS WAY?

Many mothers say they are often aware of feelings of unhappiness (anxiety, tension, and depression) as if "the world is on top of me." To help researchers understand what is happening, women were asked to discuss everything that goes on in their lives from the time they get up in the morning until they go to bed at night.

During the initial study, mothers with at least one child between the ages of five and seven were interviewed in their homes each week over a period of three to four months. They were interviewed about early life with their parents, money management, diets, work histories, and social networks. Women talked about their experiences with institutions from welfare to hospitals, from clinics to their children's schools. They also talked about their views on parenting, about their experiences of discrimination (sexual, ethnic, religious, and racial), about the men in their lives, and about their political beliefs on matters ranging from abortion regulations to local government. The women were also asked to complete mental-health questionnaires that measured symptoms of stress and depression. Each woman who participated generously shared her life experiences and knowledge. All in all, each woman provided more than five thousand separate pieces of information about her personal and community life.

Half the women in the first study were white and half were black; half were single mothers and, for comparison, half the women were currently living with a man (either a husband, lover, or friend). Because it was felt that women would be more comfortable talking with other women, no male interviewers participated either in the first study or in the second study, which was undertaken to verify the early findings and has recently been completed. This approach created very comfortable relationships, and the responses of the women interviewed were personal and open.

Women reported overwhelmingly that they had enjoyed the interview experience. Most women said it gave them a chance to reflect on their lives, to see their lives more clearly than they had before. Others said they hoped the information they shared would help other women. This book is a step in that direction.

Each woman who participated in the Stress and Families Project was promised that all information given would be kept confidential. So while the quotations, the problems, and the solutions to the problems discussed here are those of real people, all personal and place names have been changed to protect women's privacy. In addition, potentially identifying details have been altered, as well as some specific events. In places, "composite pictures" have been drawn, using the experiences of more than one woman.

COMMON CONCERNS

Many single mothers are surprised to discover the extent of their strengths, talents, and accomplishments. Expanding horizons and helping children expand theirs can be an extremely rewarding process. But when asked, women also talked about the other side of the coin: just how difficult trying to make it alone can be—what adjustments it takes to become a single mother, and how hard it is to deal with day-to-day frustrations, disappointments, and anger.

Women realized the importance of talking about their lives, of sharing common concerns as well as common joys. Out of the process of talking about experiences that millions of mothers are now sharing, many women who had felt isolated began to realize that they were not alone. Today there is no reason for any single parent to feel separated from her community and all its resources. Whatever your concern as a single parent, rest assured that other women have faced similar trials or dilemmas.

Because no two women are *exactly* alike, it is really impossible to talk about "the average mother." But millions of single mothers do share certain things in common—usually lack of time to spend on themselves the way they would like to; often not enough money to make things run evenly and smoothly. They do have more than their share of some things, but these are too often stresses and worries.

THE "FIVE MOST WANTED" LIST

Each woman brings to motherhood her own ideas about how to get the job done and her own unique experiences of life. Few women have adequate preparation for motherhood; they must rely on "on-the-job training," inventing as they go along. This approach can be especially difficult for the majority of single mothers with limited financial resources. Below are the five concerns most often cited by women as causing stress. Not surprisingly, lack of money tops the list.

1. Money: "It causes me a *great* deal of stress." "I can't seem to get as much as I need to live comfortably ... without having to worry about where my next dollar is coming from."
2. Parenting relief: "It's constant. Some days I'd give anything for a day by myself!" "There's nobody I can leave the kids with if I want to take a walk, just to get out of the house for a minute."
3. Better housing: "Just keeping warm enough to be comfortable has been a problem. All we did last winter was pay gas bills." "This apartment! When it rains it's so bad I don't have enough pans to catch all the leaks!"
4. Better relations with men: "Seems like my boyfriend is more trouble to take care of than the kids." "My ex-husband just

makes it worse. . . . He's always criticizing me about how I take care of the children."
5. A good job: "I thought working and having my daughter in school was the solution to my problem. But it isn't because I don't make enough. I can't make ends meet on a hundred and twenty-five dollars a week." "I can't even pay my babysitter. . . . I have a charge account with her."

Ongoing concerns about health matters could be added to the list as the sixth most often discussed problem area. Of course, other areas were mentioned, such as emotional insecurity and how to get reestablished in the community as single women, but those listed above are most stressful to the majority of women solo parenting in today's increasingly complex world.

No instant answers exist to most of the questions single mothers have about their lives. Most concerns are not isolated events; they are parts of an interrelated whole. So this book deals with you as a total individual—within the context of your family and your community.

Because each single mother's situation is somewhat unique, it will be easiest for *you* to decide which areas of your life present the most questions to you right now. This book is designed so that you can, for the most part, skip around to chapters of greatest interest to you this week, or this month. It is hoped, however, that each chapter will provide some insights or practical information you will find useful sooner or later.

The following chapter will give you some idea of why an overabundance of stresses is a routine part of a single mother's life, and what can put you at risk for serious problems. Chapter 3 discusses how to get your emotions back together again after separation. Chapter 4 suggests ways of preventing stress build-up and maintaining a healthy body-mind, and Chapter 5 will bring you up to date on nutrition. Chapter 6 looks at how women are pioneering new life-styles which are sometimes radically different from their mothers'. Chapter 7 will show you how to handle time more efficiently and to make the most of each minute of your day. Chapter 8 provides steps for a happier homelife, which can improve your child's self-esteem as well as your own. Day-care concerns are discussed in Chapter 9, the welfare system in Chapter 10, and love and sex for single parents in Chapter 11. If you have concerns about the world of work, Chapter 12 offers approaches for starting out, making the most of middle ground, or planning strategies for getting to the top in a chosen field.

Whether you have recently become a single parent or have been going it alone for several years, this book can help you get to know yourself a little better. It will also provide suggestions for finding the information, institutions, and other women—and men—near you who can help you get the most out of each day of your life. As you begin (or continue) exploration of yourself and your community, you will find many doors just waiting to be opened. Behind each one are new—often joyful—personal discoveries to savor and share.

CHAPTER TWO

Understanding Stress: The Single Mother's Checklist

I slept a lot, but had a lot of nightmares. After a while I got to the point where I couldn't feel anything.

I began to get angry. There was a terrible tension in the air . . . everything was so mechanical. I remember trying to control everything so I wouldn't flip out. Then one morning I picked up the rocking chair and threw it across the room. The kids were all around me. They were so scared!

—ANGELA GREEN

Some mornings Angela Green, overwhelmed with panic and frustration, feels she has reached the end of all patience. On those mornings Angela wants it "all to go away," and fantasizes about another life for herself. Her end-of-the-rope feelings are experienced by millions of single mothers all too often.

How do daily pressures mount to such an intense pitch that you can be driven to despair and displays of violence? What can these pressures do to your mental and physical health? And when are overloads most likely to happen? A look at Angela's life provides some of the anwers.

ANGELA GREEN

Angela was born in New York State and, shortly after graduating from high school, married her husband, Dave. The Greens moved to Boston, where Angela worked as a clerk with a life-insurance company for two years until the birth of her first child, Tommy. Two years later they had another child, Susie.

The Greens' marriage went smoothly for a while. Financially comfortable, they lived in an apartment that Angela liked very much. But gradually the marriage began to fall apart. When the Greens had been married nine years, and Tommy was seven and Susie five, Angela became pregnant again. Two months later, Dave walked out on Angela.

At first Dave gave Angela small amounts of money for the children each month, but it wasn't enough, and being pregnant she could not return to work. To cut expenses, Angela had to move to a smaller, cheaper apartment in a less desirable neighborhood. After she had used up the last of her small savings, she was forced to apply for Aid to Families with Dependent Children (AFDC), a humiliating experience for her.

After her baby was born and she and her husband had been separated less than a year, Dave stopped paying child support entirely. Angela, now totally dependent on AFDC payments, found herself trying to support her family on one fourth the income she had had before.

The almost two years Angela lived at poverty level on these payments was a low point in her life, as it is for many women who have to resort to government aid (see Chapter 10). But with a lot of self-motivation and other changes in her life, Angela went back to work. Because she felt a nine-to-five job would not leave her enough time for the children, she took a job waiting on tables at a local restaurant. This is what a typical morning is like for her.

* * *

"I get up each weekday morning at six. Sometimes on weekends I can sleep a little later, but Billy (the two-year-old) is usually up by then. Sometimes he'll come into my bed and play quietly until six-thirty or so, sometimes seven on Saturdays. But once he's up he won't go back to sleep, so neither can I. Susie, who's seven, and Tommy, who's nine, have to be up for school by six-thirty anyway.

"I try to get them to straighten up, and then get breakfast. That can end up being a zoo. Susie wants a scrambled egg, and when I'm halfway through cooking it, decides she wants the cereal Tommy is having. Tommy won't eat hot cereal without fruit on it, but only certain fruit—usually what I'm out of. They end up arguing, and Billy starts crying if he doesn't get cereal in his mouth immediately. He throws anything he can get his hands on. The table looks like World War Three when we're all done. Then I've got like twenty minutes to get everything back together, get their clothes on them, hair brushed, teeth brushed, nails cleaned, all that. On days I'm not too exhausted I try to get up half an hour early just to have a quiet cup of coffee for myself before it all begins.

"I found it's helpful to get their clothes ready the night before because there's so much to do in the morning. If I had to be worrying about matching socks and finding clean pants . . . it would never work.

"After Sue and Tommy leave about seven-fifteen, I have to get all of Billy's things together, pack up some toys, get myself dressed, and get Billy cleaned up to take to his sitter across town. The mornings are usually a pain because I'm trying to get a lot of things done in a hurry and Billy is into everything, drawers and cabinets, you know? He can really reach. Last week he nearly got into the bleach when I went to answer the phone. If I hadn't come back into the room then—I noticed the silence, a sure giveaway with him—I'd have been over in the emergency ward again, and I just don't need that. Two months ago Billy crashed his metal truck and his arm through my glass-fronted china cabinet and needed 18 stitches—and I needed a tranquilizer afterward.

"Kids! Sometimes I just don't know. You have to be really quick, and always listening. It seems like there just isn't a minute that you can relax, really relax and take a few minutes for yourself.

"We catch the bus about seven-thirty. I drop Billy off and then get to the restaurant about eight. I work breakfast and lunch. This way I'm usually home by three or a little after, so the kids aren't with the sitter too long. If I could work dinners I'd make better tips, but then I wouldn't be home to put the kids to bed."

NOT ENOUGH HANDS

Managing Angela's type of hectic schedule for months, without a real day off, isn't unusual for many mothers. On average, women say they have only about an hour each day to themselves—barely time to unwind, to relax, to plan, to think, to do enjoyable things without constant interruptions. And even worse, it hardly leaves time for real enjoyment of your children.

Though the problem of too little enjoyable time is one that can be improved (see Chapter 7 on time management and suggestions in Chapter 4 about healthy ways to spend personal time each day), a too-hectic single-mother schedule takes a physical toll.

The morning that Angela threw her rocking chair was pretty much like the one she described above. At that time she had been keeping up her hectic pace day after day, having recurring problems with her ex-husband, and worrying constantly about bills. Most frustrating of all, she wanted to take word-processing courses that would lead to a better-paying job. Yet every week some unexpected expense seemed to crop up to prevent her from putting much away for classes. And then that morning Angela received yet one more unexpected bill that pushed her chance at self-improvement back once again. Her control snapped.

STRESS BUILDUP: WATCHING FOR BODY SIGNS

Much of the time we take our bodies for granted, unaware of just how complex they are. Minute by minute they respond to the smallest changes in the environment. Many of these changes have to do with daily maintenance or repair work (burning calories or replacing old or damaged cells). There are so many responses and most of them are so subtle that we may never be consciously aware of them. Bodies that are calm and healthy operate like a smoothly running organization with thousands of unseen employees.

But when we have to adjust to major changes in the environment we quickly become aware of body changes. If, while walking home from the store, you were suddenly confronted by a mugger with a gun, your body would immediately gear up to defend itself against a threatening situation. Among other reactions, you would produce more adrenaline and increase your heartbeat. Your muscles would prepare for "flight or fight" as your whole body went into a kind of overdrive.

At that moment, if you were able to run ten blocks and safely escape, you would effectively use up the sudden excess energy your body provided for you. Eventually your body would return to its normal state and all would be well.

But all too often the crisis situations we encounter day by day don't allow us to respond normally, in ways that would be most healthy for our bodies. Instead of a sudden encounter with a mugger we have nagging worries about the landlord who wants his rent on time, or the baby who swallows a button, or a close relative who needs an operation—any one of many possible situations will key our bodies up for action.

Because in most situations it is impossible or undesirable either to run away or to use force as a way of coping, we are often left with the problem of getting our bodies back to normal. Often we pretend that upsetting things didn't happen, or we try to push them to the back of our minds, thinking that no resolution is possible. Sometimes it works. But often the pressures just build up.

The breaking point occurs when our bodies decide they've been asked to do an unreasonable juggling act for much too long. No predictable formula tells us exactly when stresses will overflow. Because each person is unique, some of us are able to withstand a great deal of pressure; some of us very little. But sooner or later, without some relief, even the most stoic person may find herself at the explosion stage. With many women, tensions go inward and can lead to depression or severe physical damage.

After a certain point your body will give signs that it has been too long abused and ignored—perhaps stomach pains, frequent headaches, rapid breathing, chest pains, or neck and back tension. You may notice very sweaty or very dry skin accompanying that hollow feeling in the pit of the stomach. Most likely, your body will be affected at its weakest points.

THE SINGLE MOTHER'S CHECKLIST

It is easy to see why you may not notice the earliest signs of tension that can go along with solo parenting. All too often you are probably right in the middle of doing any number of things when your body sends out early warnings.

But if you are aware of the causes of stress in your life, you can begin to work around them. The list below includes some of the things that the Stress and Families Project found likely to make your days extra tough from time to time.

Do you have:

	YES	NO
Children of preschool age?	—	—
Three or more children, especially young ones?	—	—

	YES	NO
Lack of support with child care?	——	—
Housing worries (about the safety of your home, its state of repair, your neighborhood)?	——	—
Financial difficulties (especially if these are a constant source of concern)?	——	—
Lack of a supportive person you can confide in, who will listen to problems as well as good news?	——	—
A history of financial problems when you were growing up?	——	—

If you answer yes to a few of these questions, you are probably under some stress. If you answer yes to several of them, it may mean it is time to look at your life, to see where some changes can be made in the juggling act.

Although being a single parent is not easy, you are undoubtedly already coping successfully with a great many daily events. Your coping skills, probably much more extensive than you are aware of, can be rechanneled to be even more successful in the future.

But it is also likely that some of your coping strategies may be outdated. And some may not be as effective as they could be. Throwing a rocking chair, for instance, is much better than taking frustrations out on a child; but dealing with frustrations earlier and trying to *prevent* stress buildup is certainly preferable.

Chapter 4 discusses ways of preventing buildup so you can be calmer, healthier, and more enthusiastic about approaching new situations in your personal and community life. But first it may be profitable to take a look at any emotional backlog that is slowing down your progress.

CHAPTER THREE

Reborn Single: Emotional Transitions

It's been five years since Rob left, and I still think of him. I guess in some ways I'm still waiting for him to come back.

The emotional pain that most women feel during and after a marital breakup is often one of the most traumatic experiences of a lifetime. Love lost through death or through divorce leaves lots of jagged edges.

When a relationship has been deteriorating for a long time, it may in fact already be dead before separation occurs. Sometimes, though, the break is quick and surprising. In either case, the emotional wounds can be so deep that *immediate* readjustment and laughter are simply impossible. The fact is that any loss is painful, whether of a tooth, a pet, or a favorite object. The greater the loss is felt to be (as in the case of losing a partner), the longer it may take to repair the damage.

Often a woman's turmoil is compounded by feelings of guilt over the marriage itself: "It was all my fault"; "If only I had tried harder"; "If only I had handled things better." Somehow a woman ends up feeling responsible for the survival of her marriage—as if that too were "her job," as well as having and raising the kids, managing the house, and bringing in "a little extra." And often there is guilt over the children: "It's my fault they don't have a father"; "Because of me they don't have as much as other kids." Even if these feelings are not verbalized, many women assume the bulk of blame.

But marriage is a two-way street. If separation occurs it is because it takes two to disco and two to make or break a relationship. A realistic look at the institution of marriage in the eighties can help put guilt in perspective.

MARRIAGE: AN EVOLVING INSTITUTION

Marriage, like other institutions in our society, is evolving. As with any kind of change, from clothing fashions to mores, the rate of change differs depending on where you live, being faster in urban settings and slower in rural areas. But marriage is definitely changing in many fundamental ways from what it was in our grandparents' or our parents' time.

One problem is that all aspects of marriage do not change at the same rate. Though much more is asked of marriage now, we still cling to the earlier idea that it is supposed to last a lifetime. Think of the extra baggage a couple is expected to carry today: total communication between partners, increasing parental responsibility for children's development, increasing expectations of sexual fulfillment, and many more years of combating familiarity and boredom because of increased life expectancy. When these burdens are heaped on top of all the other economic, social, and psychological burdens marriage has always had to carry, it is no wonder that a lifelong union is hard to maintain. It is not surprising that at least one out of every three married women will separate in her lifetime. And this figure could go much higher. Futurists predict that soon it will be one out of every two women.

Though we still pay lip service to traditional marriage, the traditional marriage is on the verge of extinction. Today's children are already being reared in multiparent family structures, by single parents, or in very altered forms of the two-parent unit, and other arrangements are possible in the future. So when the guilt starts piling up, it's helpful to remember that separation is, more and more, becoming the norm. Singlehood doesn't have to be a second-best alternative to traditional marriage unless you insist on seeing it that way. It is one direction in which the family unit is evolving.

Yesterday's Clothes

If you have donned the Martyr Habit and are still wearing all of yesterday's guilt, you have probably found it doesn't get you anywhere, even though it may feel perversely good on some level. Constant anger, such as placing all the blame on your former partner, can do a damaging number on you too.

This is not to deny that in the dance of love one person is often following the other's moves and that men usually take the lead. Power that is not shifted occasionally—or better yet, jointly handled—can easily result in a dominating male who threatens a woman's sense of self-esteem, her personal development, and/or her body.

After this happens, it may seem true to say, "He was impossible to live with." Often the stronger-weaker approach is a prime cause of disunity. But relationships are usually too complex for there to be one bad guy and one good guy. In many ways it doesn't matter how you got where you are today. The question is, What are you going to do about it?

Understanding the past can help to put it behind you, where it belongs.

The Trouble with Marriage

Why do marriages break apart? The following list covers some of the main causes; perhaps you can add some others.

- Inexperience and too early union
- Different growth rates between partners

- Lack of communication
- Increasing, sometimes unrealistic, expectations of a partner, or of the marriage itself
- Familiarity and boredom
- Money hassles
- Parenting pressures
- Sexual difficulties and differences
- Violence
- Alcohol and drug abuse

One common reason for a broken marriage is that the timing was off. One or both partners may have felt the need to get away from their parents, and marriage provided the vehicle. Out of the frying pan into the fire. Early marriages—before couples even know who they are or what they really want and need for themselves—make growth together difficult. Many couples are unprepared for the day-to-day routine of marriage after the first intensity of romance wears off.

The common phenomenon of couples simply growing apart has been explored by many writers, including Gail Sheehy in *Passages*. One of the points Sheehy makes is that women and men are apt to experience growth at different times in their lives. Traditionally, for example, women (especially those in middle-income brackets) are ready to explore themselves and the larger world in their late twenties or early thirties. This occurs after the last child is in school, when mothering is less vital and more personal time is available.

Men, on the other hand, may reach a crisis earlier—or later—when careers are slowing down or providing less satisfaction than anticipated. This is when the previously responsible father and husband may drive off in a van to Alaska, or leave his wife for a seventeen-year-old nymph who makes him feel young again, if only temporarily.

Familiarity and boredom; growing expectations for more complete communication (without the psychological tools for bringing this about); the confusion of changing sex roles; economic hardship and all the psychological squeezing that involves; pressures with children; sexual incompatibility; and accumulating violence and drug abuse may also be working against long-term commitments.

TRANSITION TIME: WHY IS IT SO HARD TO ADJUST?

With the rising divorce rate in America more and more women are experiencing single-woman/single-parent life-styles. Those who adapt most readily to singlehood will, obviously, be those who make the most satisfying lives for themselves and their children.

Why do some women fail to make the necessary transition from marriage to successful singlehood? Though women are increasingly making it into the winner's circle, some still either hug home base for dear life or continue to fly away from their lives as if singleness were a disease. What distinguishes the winners from the losers?

The process of transition is accomplished in steps. Even if a marriage was a very destructive one, partners mourn the loss of the ideal relationship they thought they had. (This is especially likely in the case of death; widows tend to remember *only* the good things.) The steps of adjustment often begin with denial that loss has occurred. After a time, a woman progresses through anger and resentment, and through sadness and frustration felt in connection with the lost relationship, before complete adjustment occurs. Sometimes women get caught at one stage or another, and the healing process is slowed by unresolved emotions.

Hide 'n' Seek

Two paths are common immediately after separation. A woman may retreat into her mothering role and her home, closing off needs for intimacy and male contact. Or she may drown the pain and confusion of separation in rounds of activities and/or other men.

Such extremes are a part of survival. Everyone needs to put up some defenses now and then; it is like building barricades against an invading enemy—in this case, pain and confusion. These barriers can serve their purpose. But the more defenses we erect, the harder it will be to get rid of them when their usefulness has passed. Eventually we may even forget we put them up, leading them to become permanent fixtures, obstructions to healthy behavior. Long-held defenses tend to take on a life of their own, and getting rid of them may be like trying to dismantle the Great Wall of China.

A healthier alternative is sought eventually—midway between these extremes—combining some immediate personal space and healing time with a reasonable amount of social contact. How long it is likely to take a woman to reach this middle ground depends on a number of things, including:

• Her level of self-esteem
• The number and kinds of options available
• The amount of support she finds from her friends, family, and the larger community
• How intensely she may love and/or hate her ex-husband.

Women have remarkable stores of energy and resilience; we have to! And sooner or later the scars begin to heal and optimism takes over. But the deeper our wounds have been, the longer they take to close. For women who feel powerless, who have few options at the time of separation, healing may be especially slow. The more real options you have as a woman, the less likely you are (at any time) to cling to one man as if he were your life raft. So it is very important to find and create as many options for yourself as you can.

Breaking the Habit
Habit is probably the greatest peril, in relationships and in other aspects of life. Love, for instance, may get you into a marriage, but it is often habit that keeps you there. Even if your morning coffee was accompanied by alienating silence or

recurrent arguments with your partner, at least you knew the patterns of your life. And you didn't know what would happen if those habits were discontinued.

This fear of change can be equally overwhelming after separation. It can keep you sitting at home with *Love Boat* thirty-two Saturday nights in a row. It is easy to convert the habit of morning argument over breakfast to an equally wasteful one of TV watching.

Breaking the limited image of the women we are, and what we can accomplish, is hard to do. It sometimes means taking risks, meeting new people, trying for another job, volunteering for an office in your club. The easiest way to begin is to try one new thing a week—one small but new option you never had as part of a couple. Ask yourself how you are benefiting from your independence, or if it is now being wasted. Whether you try a new recipe, meet a new neighbor for coffee, or take a golf lesson, explore something different each week, to keep you vital and growing. Staying the same forever, safe as that may seem to be, is deadening.

Emotional Quicksand

Transition from wife to independent, confident woman is sometimes slowed by emotional turmoil. If your relationship had been going downhill gradually, you may have eroded your self-confidence over months or years of futile attempts to patch up the whole mess. Now you are caught in the quicksand of seeing yourself as incompetent or undesirable.

This is especially likely if your former partner was overtly domineering or, as in the case of drug addicts, hypochondriacs, and alcoholics, highly manipulative. Some women (and men) end relationships only after years of emotional or physical battering by spouses, which leaves their egos much reduced in size. And when you are feeling two feet tall it is hard, once you are free, to do a quick about-face and think of yourself as strong, inquisitive, or self-reliant.

To make matters more difficult, women are *still* finding unequal access to money in the workplace. Aware of the limited options that may be available, many women feel a realistic apprehension of singlehood. This is not surprising when you consider that millions of women enter marriage and/or motherhood before they have had experience working and living on their own. And after marriage many women leave banking, insurance, and finances to their husbands. In these cases, the prospect of making it on their own—let alone supporting a family—can make them feel as if they are perched on the edge of an abyss.

CHANGING FOCUS: REBORN SINGLE

Whether in suburbs or in the confines of urban apartment blocks, many married women have experienced what they describe as a slow erosion of identity. With child-care responsibilities from morning to night, they are frequently isolated—and their sole or chief contact with "the outside world" comes through their husbands. Life is sometimes lived vicariously in marriage: Information is gathered from dinner-table conversation or the six o'clock news.

As a single parent you are not living life at second hand anymore. That is one of the exciting things about it. But separation may have brought with it a sudden awareness of your ignorance. As you once had little idea of what marriage would entail, so singlehood can seem a huge unknown.

If you worked prior to marriage and motherhood, the transition to single parent may be smoother than if you had little or no work experience. You know that you once made your own connections with the world "out there," that you probably did it quite well and can do it again.

But even if you have never had much opportunity before, the chances are that now—with more life experience and greater determination—you will do a better job than you might have earlier in life. Time and time again your own strengths will surprise you, as many women interviewed in the Stress and Families Project have testified.

Making It

Relieved of the burden of another adult to worry about, many women quickly rechannel their energies into their own lives, with astonishing results. They lead lives they never would have thought possible, and that in fact they might never have achieved had they remained married.

Overcoming your natural fears is easier if you realize that all separated women (millions each year) have had to come to grips with similar fears of loneliness, lack of money, or too much responsibility. Some fly high; some don't make it quite so far off the ground. Reentry into the marketplace is discussed in Chapter 12, but first you must achieve reentry into your own private mind space and home space, and begin to bring your new image into focus. You are an evolving woman. How do you make the most of who you are becoming?

Without some plan of action, you may grope around in the confusion of transition for too long. To establish a firm base, five things are necessary. Some of these you may have handled already; some you may not. To put the past to bed and get on with your new present you need to:

- Accept that change is here; "you can't go home again";
- Acknowledge the need for a little time to mourn the past and readjust to your new situation;
- Concentrate on your positive options; refuse to fall back on fears and self-pity;
- Take an inventory of your assets;
- Set singlehood goals immediately, both short-term and long-term.

Accepting Loss and Change

All changes require some adjusting. Often changes are so trivial that we can easily adapt: Your gas bill has gone up five dollars; the shampoo you normally buy has gone off the market; Bobby breaks his shoelaces and you have to get new ones. Our reaction to such mundane changes is to adjust automatically without giving the matter much thought or planning.

Larger or more unusual changes—death of a parent, moving to a new neighborhood, a decrease in income, sickness—are more likely to involve conscious coping skills. Becoming a single woman often involves several major changes at once. Divorce can lead to a shift in home and income, a different school for your child, and of course, an adjustment to relying on yourself instead of on the man who is no longer sitting down at the dinner table with you.

Adjusting to the physical changes in your life will probably keep you very busy for a while. Then you may go through a period of denial. Perhaps you can cover your emotional turmoil effectively for some time—hermiting away in your bedroom Saturday nights with a series of Gothic romances or hitting every dating bar in town. But at some point you will have to take a good look at the life—and the woman—you left behind.

No longer do you see yourself as "wife of . . ."; you are now Mary Smith, Delia Jones, or Jane Rosenberg. But before you can appreciate and accept this new woman, you must say good-bye to some pieces of the past. As with any major loss, some mourning time occurs as an early phase of the healing process.

Anger and sadness are natural emotions under the circumstances, and they need to be expressed. But sometimes we can get stuck in self-pity. Not only does it hurt and/or bore others at this point, it considerably slows down the process of reaching new life goals and balance.

Letting Go

Clinging to the past is the surest, quickest way to let your life slide through your fingers. Some women still lament their former lives a decade or more after the divorce decree has been mailed out. Often they romanticize the past until it is an unrecognizable inflation of what was never an ideal situation.

For women who have been coupled for a long time, it is

tempting to think that "someday Joe will come back, a new, repentant man." While there is an outside chance that this may happen, in all likelihood it won't. And what's more, you probably wouldn't be happy with him the second time around even if he appeared on your doorstep tomorrow.

Finding little excuses to get in touch with your ex ("I just called because the porch step came loose again"; "The car is making a strange noise"; "Billy's teacher yelled at him yesterday") rarely provides anything but more heartbreak and lowered self-esteem. Instead of waiting for him to fix things, you'll feel a lot better emotionally and a lot more competent if you fix them yourself.

In each such instance, instead of hoping to resurrect the ghosts of your former life, take one small but definite step away from dependency. Buy a hammer and nail the porch step, ask an auto mechanic what is wrong with the car, or deal with Billy's teacher yourself. Immediately. And plan on taking one more independent step next week and the week after. Each independent act will add to your sense of survival.

Expression: Productive Mourning

Accepting your right to feel occasional surges of hurt and anger is important. Expressing those feelings, and getting reinforcement for the new paths you are taking, is equally important. You don't need to go around in a fury for years. But airing opinions and feelings productively (with friends, a support group of women dealing with similar issues, or even with a good, short-term therapist) helps resolve issues more quickly than bouncing them off the walls of your head.

A circle of other single women will quickly make you realize that you are not the first to remake a self-image; you are only one of millions of women who has had to build again. If you are a good listener and ready to look for new pathways, other women can also give you some clues on successfully resolving the issues you need to work through. You may be getting all the support you need from family, friends, or neighbors. But if you feel you aren't, consider getting some friends together for a weekly discussion group, or check your paper for ongoing support groups that are dealing with a particular issue you want to explore.

Reality Checking: What Was Missing?

Also helpful is a realistic assessment of what was missing in your past. Without some objective analysis, it is all too easy to repeat the same mistakes a second time around.

When you fondly begin to replay "the good times," reminiscence can act like a drug, clouding over the truth. Did you really have a knight in shining armor who handled all dragons with great dispatch and got home on a run to sweep you into his arms? Maybe your former relationship was not all that bad and you became a single woman because your husband opted out. Maybe he never hit you and he remembered flowers on your birthday. But most likely you were not living with Lancelot.

What drove you crazy? Did he ever *really* listen and understand? Was his head always behind the newspaper or turned to football games when you were trying to communicate something important? Did he make it to the PTA meetings with you, or go to the kids' school events? Was he often down about you and life? Could he vastly have improved his lovemaking, or was it more of the same old sex? Did you really love picking up his socks and making all meals the same old boring way he liked them? No man is perfect. And clinging to unrealistic images, in those moments when you are afraid of the dark or the future, only adds one more ghost to the household, and an inflated ghost at that.

Finding the Patterns

It's likely you are going to meet a lot of men in your new life. Before getting into another intimate involvement, however, it's only sensible to see the pitfalls of the last one so you can avoid falling into the same old pattern. Do you know what your patterns are? Do you know what attracts you to particular men? Can you quickly spot healthy behavior and unhealthy, potentially damaging actions?

Women often expect from their partners what they have known in the past. What our mothers had, whatever is typical of behavior around us—this is often what we shoot for. As men are often unconsciously looking for a woman who reminds them of Mom, women often find younger versions of Pop.

If your father was a nice, loving, and sensitive guy, then everything may be OK. But was he? And was your former partner like him in too many ways that are incompatible with the evolving woman you are?

Ms. Nathan, for example, did not really question what she was looking for in a man until she found herself about to enter her third living arrangement. Like her two previous men, this one was a businessman who was a workaholic and prone to physical violence under stress. By that time she had an ulcer and three broken ribs. In her choice of men, she had kept the pattern in motion; it was her own pattern that was causing the damage.

Maybe your ex spent every spare minute with the boys; maybe he simply could not communicate emotionally; maybe he automatically turned into Casanova at parties and you were never quite sure where he was when he wasn't with you. What were his patterns and how did you deal with them? Do you want to repeat the same frustrations the next time around? If you feel you have some negative conditioning to work through, don't be in a hurry to give up the independence you're working so hard to achieve.

ACCENTING THE POSITIVE

For many women, becoming single is a very scary process, as we have seen. But for others, singleness comes like a breath of fresh air, or like the ending of a years-long migraine; there is immense relief from pain. Women often say that after the initial adjustments from wife to independent woman, they experience freedoms that make their current lives a natural high.

Concentrating on the positive aspects of singleness each day helps keep these women healthy and growing while some of their sisters are still caught in the webs of the past. Rather than dwelling on what you don't have, try reminding yourself of what life has to offer. The blessings often far outweigh the hardships. It is just a matter of correcting your vision, like buying a new pair of glasses.

Space Exploration

Like many women, before becoming a single mother you may never have owned your own space, either physical or emotional. Space, like money, is a resource. It means having a secure place to be, a place you can make comfortable in any way you like, whether by adding flowers to the table or African mats to the floor. It is a sanctuary that any woman needs after coming through the battleground of separation.

Women accenting the positive events of new lives make daily discoveries of things that were missing before they had a sanctuary. They make the most of their space once they are relieved of the constant drains of bad relationships.

Three forms of drain are all too common in many marriages: emotional, psychological, and physical. When these abuses are combined over a long period of time, the personality can actually suffer a sense of reduction, rather like the Incredible Shrinking Man. But humans are remarkably resilient. Once they are taken out of an unhealthy environment, new growth can start quickly, as plants reach for the sun after being neglected in dark corners.

Physical Space: No More Fear

For women who have been physically abused in marriage, the freedom of personal physical space provides great relief: Being alone is being safe. Violence is not a new disease in America. It is not a new disease in history. Violence is known among all classes, worldwide. The first experience is always terrifying, humiliating, and painful. The long-term effects can be devastating to a woman's personality.

Roberta Parker is one of many women who is thankful daily for a sanctuary where she and her children feel safe. Roberta is an average-sized woman, a little on the slender side, pretty and soft-spoken. While unique in many ways, she shares one thing with millions of other women. She was, during the eight years of her marriage, periodically beaten by her husband. This is how it felt: "I was constantly in a state of fear. I got steadily sicker and sicker, lost weight drastically and had to get my gallbladder out. My jaw won't ever be the same again. Emotionally I got so full of fear I couldn't talk on the phone or go out of the house in case he called and I wasn't there. I jumped a lot—at nothing at all."

Why Do They Stay?   Women who have never been physically abused find it hard to understand why women stay in homes where the likelihood of recurring violence is high. As is usual in decision making, staying usually involves a pattern of reasons, not just one. Here are some of the reasons they give.

• For the sake of the children
• Having nowhere else to go
• Believing it won't happen again
• Feeling to blame because "I didn't handle things right"
• Feeling violence is deserved
• Fear of being killed if escape is attempted
• Thinking violence is a man's "natural reaction"

For many mothers, the answer is that they simply have nowhere else to go. They may be economically and/or psychologically dependent, and the question is further complicated by the presence of children. Often a man is physically abusive to all or many family members, but sometimes he directs his violence primarily against his wife. Children may have divided affection in this case simply because he is their father, or because they have not been on the receiving end of his fist.

Often too, women are simply stunned the first time a beating occurs and have an overwhelming desire to believe the black eye was an accident that won't happen again. Husbands are usually repentant afterward and promise good behavior in the future. But statistics show that once a man is physically abusive he is much more likely to be so again, rather than looking for help in dealing with his problems in healthier ways.

If you have separated because of violence, feel assured you have made a wise decision. Quite possibly, the next time around you might have been seriously injured. The thing to do at this point—even if you have to harden your heart to do it— is to make sure it never happens again. Remembering that it is *his* problem, not yours, can help. As one woman put it, "I thought if I could just balance things out, keep him somehow on an even keel, it would be all right. I ended up tiptoeing around as if I were walking on eggs all the time. It made me a nervous wreck. Now I know there was nothing I could have done."

Saying NO: While violence is not a new phenomenon, what is new is that women in increasing numbers are saying no to home victimization. Growing economic opportunities (slow as they are on some fronts), relaxed divorce laws and fewer taboos on discussion of male violence, and women's communications networks help provide options to a lifetime of abuse.

Sometimes sharing the experience with a friend or relative relieves some of the pain, and helps put things into perspective. But sometimes the experiences of brutality take a long time to heal. If you have been subjected to physical violence and it is still bothering you, or you are tempted to pass it on to your children, you need to explore the issue further before you can let go of it. You may need help in working through the anger that is a natural accompaniment to victimization. Temporary homes and shelters for battered women are springing up all over the nation, along with discussion groups and specialized counselors available by calling hotlines, women's centers, parents' support groups, and sometimes local hospitals.

Emotional Space

Physical space can be gratifying enough for some women who have seen heavy combat. But having emotional space often comes as a huge relief as well. It is relief from the constant negative voice in the ear ("He used to tell me I was stupid all the time"; "When he got mad he'd call me every name in the book").

Some echoes may remain even years after separation. The last negative messages you received from your ex can take hold all too easily in your own mind if they aren't weeded out. And sometimes we repeat them, making those negatives part of who we think we are. To sort this out, the next time you find yourself mentally criticizing something you've done—or haven't done—ask where in your past the negative ideas originated. Do they really fit the woman you are and the woman you are becoming? To use your emotional space well, make sure you are filling it with very postitive images of yourself and who you want to be, not with the names someone else has hung on you. It helps to surround yourself with positive others— people who support and appreciate your efforts to make your new life a good one.

PERSONAL INVENTORY

To maintain a positive image, it helps to make a private list— an inventory to which you can refer and to which you add items periodically. Include in it all the positive things you have in your life right now, especially those that weren't there before you became a single woman. Drawing up such a list will help you see many wonderful things about your life that you'd overlooked in your concern over what's been missing. Even if you consider yourself an experienced single mother, take ten or fifteen minutes to complete this exercise. It really is effective. The first few items will probably be obvious things you've been vaguely aware of for some time. But as you keep searching, you'll dredge up some gems that will surprise you. Making lists forces us to marshall our thoughts in a more orderly, objective manner. And it's an easy and inexpensive form of amateur psychoanalysis. Taking these exercises seriously can lead to numerous self-discoveries.

Your list may include some things that are valued by millions of other single women, but it will undoubtedly include your own personal treasures as well. The following special blessings were among those mentioned by women interviewed by the Stress and Families Project:

Freedom from being "second best." "My ex-husband always used to make me feel like my life wasn't as important as his."

Meeting new people. "He really wasn't comfortable with people. Now that he's gone I meet new people all the time; some of them are becoming very good friends."

No more negativity. "He was always complaining about everything, from how I cooked the pork chops to what I wore when we went out."

Freedom of choice. "Even though I'd like to get out more, when I am out it's my time. When I was married I used to end up doing just what he wanted all the time, and never going where I wanted to go."

Less boredom. "I wouldn't say my life is always happy, but I'm certainly not bored. Every day is a new experience for me."

Doing the postponed. "I started taking dance classes, something I'd been wanting to do for years. And I love it!"

Exploring new skills and talents. "I never did the bills while we were married; I didn't even know how much money we had. I'm really proud of how well I handle money now."

Personal sexual freedom. "I didn't know what I was doing before I got married and I never really enjoyed sex a lot. I've discovered all men aren't like he was. When I think of what I was missing all those years!"

GOAL SETTING

Once you have completed a "goods inventory," make a list of what you feel is missing from singlehood as you are now living it. Single mothers most often mention a need for material goods (better housing, more income, more help with child care, etc.) as well as for satisfying male relations. Your list might include things like the following:

- A nicer apartment
- A higher-paying or more interesting job
- More money to pay for: better schooling for the kids; some dinners out at nice restaurants every now and then; a newer car, or just a car period; nicer clothes; vacations
- More education
- Male companionship or enough good sex

As well as the basics like more steak dinners and freedom from worry about bills, include inexpensive whim items and dream items too, even if they sound silly or farfetched. If you have always had a secret yearning to go to Hawaii, put that on your list. If you never got the birthstone ring you always wanted, add that too.

Once you have listed everything that you feel is missing right now, whether a necessity for your immediate happiness or a whim item, rank them in order of importance. List the most essential items first; end with those things that you are willing to wait longer for.

Now pick one item from the essentials and write that goal on a piece of paper. Think about it. Tape the goal on your refrigerator so that you can keep asking yourself what you need to do to make that goal come true. If, for instance, you really hate the neighborhood you are in right now, ask yourself where you would rather live, and how long it will take you to get there. Think in specifics—a nicer section of town or a particular apartment building.

Visualize yourself in that apartment building and hold that image in your head for a few minutes. Why can't you live there? List each barrier to attaining that goal and each possible solution you can think of. (There may be many more that will occur to you in the weeks to come.) If, for example, you know that rents in that building are a hundred dollars more a month than what you are now paying, you calculate that you would need an extra twelve hundred dollars a year to live there. How can you get that money? And how long will it take? Is it possible to cut something out of your present expenses, like a car? Can you eliminate something less important for something more important?

If reducing expenses is not possible, then you're going to have to add some income—and this is where you may have to detour a bit. Maybe your first goal should be a better-paying job. But keeping that apartment in mind may provide enough incentive to find another job. Sound difficult? Goals often are; but it's better to reach for them than to keep saying it's impossible. If you try for that apartment now, keeping at it and setting a time limit for getting it, it's highly likely you will have it in a year, or two, or three. If you don't try for it, it will always remain an "Oh, I wish . . ."—just a dream.

Once you have decided on your first long-term goal, go back to your list and pick a short-term goal, one you can accomplish in a week. Maybe you decided long ago to try a permanent. Make an appointment today and keep it. Perhaps you could really use a kitchen bulletin board as an all-round organizer to keep track of weekly chores, phone messages, etc. Set some money aside, buy the board within a week, and fix it up just the way you want it. Short-term goals can sometimes require little or no money. Maybe you've been meaning for months to strip the old paint off that funny little table you picked up in a yard sale last summer. Figure out how long it will take, working on it evenings or part of Saturday or Sunday, and get it done within seven days. Set a reasonable time limit for each short-term goal you make—at least one a month.

Short-term goal setting gives us practice in focusing our energy into accomplishments and adds to our self-esteem. Also, once we meet these goals, they are visible signs of our ability to organize our time. They give us a definite sense of accomplishment, and an idea of how the goal-setting process works. They also tide over our satisfaction needs as we continue applying energy to our long-term goals.

Unfortunately, while men are used to goal setting—indeed, on executive levels they are often specifically trained in setting goals—women are seldom taught to go out and get. In addition women are often made to feel unfeminine for doing more than waiting for what comes along. White women could benefit from black women's experience in this respect. Since black men have, historically, been denied access to better-paying jobs, many black women never grew up with the "kept woman" dream. This doesn't mean that black women haven't also been put down for being "aggressive" (read self-reliant). They just may have had to break through some of the self-destructive myths of femininity a little earlier in life.

Only you can re-create a more honest and positive view of who you are and what your needs are. And only you can make your life goals a possibility. But once you begin to set goals in your life, you will probably be amazed to discover how many of the things you want are attainable.

References
DeRosis, Helen, and Victoria Pellegrino. *The Book of Hope.** New York: Bantam Books, 1976.
Sheehy, Gail. *Passages.* New York: Bantam Books, 1977.

*Recommended

CHAPTER FOUR

Body Basics:
The VIP Treatment

When I got to work on Monday I could feel myself getting tensed and choked up. I took a tranquilizer but it didn't do anything, so I took another. Then I got really dizzy and knew I had to get to the hospital.

By the time a friend got me there I was too weak to get out of the car. They had to get a wheelchair for me. It was only after that I started thinking about how I'd been neglecting myself. I had to take a really good look at my life, and what was happening to my body.

—PAT COLLINS

How does your body feel to you right now? And how does it look? As you sit, is your spine straight, your breathing even, your muscles pleasantly relaxed? Or do you slump and sag in your chair, feeling rather like a bag of unevenly distributed groceries?

If you are like many single mothers you may hardly have a chance to think about your body in the course of the day. You may take your body for granted—for hectic days or even weeks on end—until you suddenly discover just how much tension has been building up in your shoulders, stomach, back, or neck.

Probably you are taking better care of your body than Pat Collins was and have never experienced the total body distress and panic she felt when she found herself in the emergency ward of her local hospital. But what are you doing to keep your body as beautiful and healthy as it can possibly be?

Pat's emergency shocked her into realizing the toll her life-style was taking on her body, and how overload can sneak up when not enough attention is paid to body basics. Pat had to take a good thorough look at where she was headed. And then she had to make some changes in her life. Some of the changes she made involve techniques that can prove helpful to any woman who is solo parenting without a routine program of personal care—one aimed at a healthier, crisis-prevention way of life.

HEALING YESTERDAY'S BATTLE FATIGUE

Our bodies can be abused in any one of thousands of ways and most of the time they will miraculously build new cells and heal themselves. This automatic repair process can happen, however, only when we give our bodies what they need to do the job. Nutritious food and time for rest and rebuilding are two necessary ingredients. Unfortunately, single mothers are often short of both. When a person is deprived of essential body basics long enough, chronic health problems often result.

If you know, or suspect, you have a stress-aggravated condition, you are not alone. A number of women interviewed by the Stress and Families Project were found to be experiencing such conditions as part of what can be called the "stressed mothers syndrome:"[1]

- Asthma or other respiratory problems
- Arthritis, bursitis, or other pain related to joints and muscles (back and neck pains are particularly common)

- Intestinal problems such as spastic colon
- Frequent headaches or migraines
- Skin conditions: dry skin, red patching, or psoriasis
- Frequent stomach discomfort, indigestion, or even ulcers

These conditions may be accompanied by general signs of depletion or overstimulation:

- Chronic exhaustion (as if you were always one or two days behind in your sleep)
- Daily bouts of "nerves"—feeling that you are being stretched in at least four different directions at the same time

If you recognize the symptoms and have been ignoring them, you should, of course, seek treatment as soon as possible. *Our Bodies, Ourselves* by the Boston Women's Health Book Collective offers help in choosing a good doctor if you don't already have one, or for becoming a more informed health consumer with the doctor you already have. *Bodies* is also an excellent reference source for general health and body information—a must for every woman's shelf.

The good news is that most of these conditions can be improved or eliminated with some minor changes in life-style. And with a little consistent attention, you can make sure that they don't recur in the future.

The bonus is that your children will also feel better. Research studies have demonstrated that when mothers feel good about themselves their children are also more satisfied with life. That makes sense. What happens to one member of a family circle affects the other individuals. So the more good feelings you feed into your circle the stronger it is going to be. A healthy, energetic body-mind will help you accomplish things you never dreamed you could.

Getting back in touch with your body in a thoughtful, positive way can make all the difference in the world. Yet it doesn't necessarily take more money or a total change in habits. As Pat Collins said:

"It's funny; I'm not living all that differently than before. I'm just living, I guess, more thoughtfully about myself. I'm trying to fit me and my needs into my life. And that's something I just wasn't doing before. I'm taking care of my body in little ways. I feel good, and I find I'm laughing again. Friends say I look a lot younger."

Step 1: The VIP Treatment

The first step is simple but effective. Every day when you wake up, say to yourself: "I am a Very Important Person." Pat Collins found out how this little formula actually works. For a long time (many years, in fact) Pat had put everyone else in the world first: her children, her ex-husband, her mother, her poor sick aunt, her friends, even the dog. Putting everyone else first was nice—in a way; it allowed Pat the good feelings of giving. But what happens when loving care flows only one way and no one is giving back?

Too much going out and not enough coming in spells depletion. And Pat had reached that point. Unfortunately, she hadn't realized she was running dry until she found herself in the hospital.

As part of her cure, Pat had to put herself at the top of the list of people to take care of. It took a while, but soon the damage her body had sustained began to heal. It was a hard but valuable lesson. Now, Pat says, she has learned to make sure her body gets what it needs to keep going "on top of the world instead of hauling the world around on top of me."

Every day now Pat reminds herself she is a VIP. She actually tells herself this, out loud, every day. And she treats herself like a very important person too. Pat makes sure that she gets enough rest and relaxation time. She eats more nourishing, less rushed meals, and she even treats herself to little personal rewards periodically—a new hair conditioner, scented candles, or a bottle of her favorite wine. These are reminders of how well she has managed to straighten out her life priorities. The changes didn't take a lot of time or money—just remembering how important she is, and what happens when she forgets that.

For Pat, attitude is more than half the battle. Previously, whenever she put herself last it was like telling herself, "I don't deserve good treatment." Now, thinking and speaking positively about herself has paid off.

However, once you start reminding yourself each day that you are a VIP, you may begin to hear voices: from a relative, a lover or a friend, a neighbor who says, "Well, that's fine, if you want to be selfish."

Leap over such people as quickly as you can: They are probably anxious about losing some of the attention you have been lavishing in their direction. Remind them that there is a *big* difference between selfishness and self-respect.

Your children may also resent the little pockets of time you are going to start devoting to your own health needs, but be firm. Let them know that if you feel good you are going to have more love to spread around. You have two jobs to do. And you can't take care of either properly if you aren't in the very best shape.

Step 2: Daily Diagnosis—Mind, Body, or the Weather?

Once you have begun to *think* about yourself as a VIP (repeating the words right now, and every morning and evening for at least two weeks), you will want to *feel* like one. The place to start your body work is with a daily self-diagnosis. When you wake up each morning ask yourself, "How do I feel?" Imagine a one- to ten-point scale, where ten means that you couldn't feel better, you are just a step away from flying; one means that you feel so out of balance you find it hard to move; five is the middle point (not great, but not terrible; OK).

On those days when you are hitting the high numbers, ask yourself what you have been doing lately that makes you feel so good—and do more of it. Did you have an especially good night's sleep or treat yourself to lunch out with a friend? Are you finding a little more satisfaction in a new job, or feeling good about that dance class you started? Whatever the cause, locate it, and try to find out why it makes you feel good. If you can, repeat it to see if it works again.

On those days when you're edging below a middle point of five, try to pinpoint those things that have sent you sliding downward. Maybe you are worrying about the rent, or had a fight with your mother, or spent too many nights in a row at home with the kids and the TV. Again, locate the cause, if possible.

Sometimes an obvious cause of a two- or three-day low is hard to pinpoint. The rent is paid, work is going well, the children are harmonizing, but you aren't. What's happening? It may be just a downward swing in your own personal pattern (called a biorhythmic cycle), or even your reaction to the weather or phases of the moon—some doctors have noted that the full or new moon can affect our sense of emotional well being.

Often a low is influenced by the accumulated stresses of solo parenting. If they are piling up, it's likely you're not getting enough of your nine basic body needs satisfied.

STEP BY STEP

When was the last time you made sure you had:

1. Some QMT (Quiet Morning Time to begin your day);
2. High-Nutrient Food (three nourishing, unhurried meals a day);
3. A Midday Body-Toning Break;
4. PCE (Positive Communication Exchange with other adults);
5. Play Time (as necessary for you as for your children);
6. A Safe Stress Outlet (a "pillow pounding," brisk exercise, or other diversion that allows you an outlet for accumulated tensions and anger);
7. A Love Session (concentrated, tender loving body care);
8. A Consciousness Cleansing (planned time to give your brain a break, to shut out the daily noises and tune in to something especially soothing);
9. At least eight hours of healing, relaxed sleep?

There is no denying that having a lot of money would make it easier to assure that these nine needs are met. You could afford mini-vacations, dinners out, expensive entertainments, and hired help with housekeeping and child care—all the cushions that make life a lot smoother. But even on a limited budget, a` VIP can find ways to make mothering a healthier occupation. One of these is by thinking prevention instead of crisis management.

Learning how to bring your body up to a good, strong level, and to keep it there, is worth a thousand pills after a stress-caused medical condition has developed. Some doctors are now including prevention advice as part of their treatment for people with high-stress life-styles. Using prevention of medical problems as a goal in your own and your children's lives can help avoid expensive doctor bills and health crises. How can you begin?

1. QMT—Quiet Morning Time

This should be the first item on each single mother's agenda. Set aside the first ten to fifteen minutes of each day (thirty if you can manage it) for you alone. With all the things you have on your mind, the beginning of each day should include a little "gathering time," time to sit quietly and get yourself together and prepare for the next twelve to sixteen hours.

How you set the mood and pace of each day is very important. Waking to cries for food and attention, to the blaring of a television, and to all the other demands of early morning is a sure way to end up with tension before you even get out the door.

Finding Quiet Morning Time daily is difficult for almost any single mother, and especially difficult if you have small children. But it isn't impossible. Chapter 7 provides tips on time management that should allow you to include QMT for yourself on a routine basis with minimal struggle. After a week or so you will probably wonder how you ever lived without it.

To make the most of this morning time you might want to try:

- A warm shower or brisk wet-towel rubbing all over your body to get your circulation going
- Two or three minutes of gentle wake-up exercise and/or
- A few minutes of "breath control"

After you are awake and loosened up, find the quietest spot in your home—not necessarily the most comfortable or you might fall asleep again. Sit cross-legged (Indian style) on the floor (if that is relaxing for you) or in a straight-backed chair with your spine and neck in alignment and your feet flat on the floor and about a foot apart. Breathe in as slowly as you can to the count of seven. Hold that breath for a count of one and, just as gradually, release your breath, again to the count of seven.

Do this at least ten times or, if you prefer, work up to a slow breath count of twenty-one. As you breathe, clear your head of everything. Concentrate on your breathing only. Feel the air coming into your lungs, expanding them, and filling your chest. Feel the air going out and with it all negative thoughts.

If you have ever taken a course in yoga you will be aware that "learning to breathe" is one of the most important steps you can take toward good health and feelings of well-being. Breathing is one of the first things to be affected by tension and emotion. Erratic breathing prevents a proper flow of oxygen and can lead to body malfunction.

For the first week, do your breathing exercise for just two minutes. Gradually work up to five or ten minutes. Try not to think of what you have to do, or of anything upsetting. Just let your breathing happen. Thoughts will intrude at first. That is normal. But every time you start to worry, or to think about packing lunches or about unpaid bills, go back to your breathing and clear your head.

On mornings when you are running late and must skip some part of your morning routine, don't skip this exercise if at all possible. You will find that even a few minutes a day can increase your overall calm and improve your ability to concentrate. And after a few months you will find that in moments of panic or high tension you should be able to slip at will into the calm center you find by practicing breathing control.

2. High-Nutrient Food

Your body is constantly rebuilding itself with the building blocks you feed into your system. To some extent, the shape and texture and strength of the resulting "building" depends on the foods you eat and the liquids you drink. In a very real way, you are what you eat.

To help your body become its most beautiful, you don't have to become a nutrition expert, haunt the health-food stores, or spend ten hours a day cooking. You just have to know which foods provide the most energy and nutrients at the least cost. Some of the best-tasting and most nourishing foods available—whole grains, fish, fresh fruits, cheeses and other dairy products, and a host of vegetables—can be combined into the least expensive and quickest meals. A growing variety of soybean products, which provide high amounts of concentrated protein—at far less cost than meat—can be cooked in dishes like lasagna and spaghetti sauce or made into "burgers," with great results!

Generally, the less foods are cooked, the more they retain their good vitamins and minerals. The more foods are processed—precooked, or canned, bottled, or frozen—the more nutrients they lose, and the less they have to offer you in fuel and building blocks. Chapter 12 will provide you with the information you need to brush up on nutritional basics.

3. Body Toning

As a single mother, you will find your body is undoubtedly in motion more than at rest. Some mothers feel they are ready for the Olympics with all the exercise they get; but what kind of exercise is it? Rushing to your second job, the bus stop, or the dentist; lugging children, hauling laundry, or washing yet more dishes? You may be clocking a lot of miles but your movements are probably stop and go—the kind of movements that do more to strain and tire out your body than to improve your circulation and build strength where you really need it. Like a car constantly driven in heavy traffic, sooner or later you will feel ready for a ten-thousand mile tune-up.

Any number of toning techniques can be used to get your body smoothly back into gear. And midday is a good time to do it. If you are at work and free from child-care responsibilities, take a brisk walk with a co-worker, followed by five or ten minutes of exercise in a lounge, or an empty office. Even a few feet of quiet hallway might do if no other space is available to you.

When possible, and desirable, invite co-workers to join in— this could lead to finding a permanent space available at your workplace, or to the beginning of a lunchtime dance group. Dance groups can be less structured than regular exercise classes but just as effective, since your whole body is kept in motion. It's likely that someone has a radio or cassette recorder she'd be willing to bring in to get a group started. Having others to exercise with is more fun and also makes it easier to stick to a resolution of routine exercise.

If exercise is simply impossible at your place of work, you might investigate other opportunities for a midday change of pace. Arlene Dinaro, a medical secretary, joined a nearby YWCA where, for a moderate fee, she swims during her lunch hour. In addition to improving body firmness, swimming got Arlene away from the expensive restaurants she was frequenting with her co-workers. Another woman joined a local exercise salon just down the street from her employer's building and manages to get away from her hectic office job for thirty-minute workouts.

If you are at home at midday, try to find a televised exercise class. Or find one that is aired early in the day and tune in before breakfast to add some pep to those mornings when you are really dragging. Create your own exercise routine. Without the restrictions of a nine-to-five schedule, you should have more potential free time each day to put on a record or two (a good fast set of disco or rock) and dance away the day's tensions and extra calories. For at-home mothers, as with out-of-the-home mothers, finding someone to share this time will help ensure exercise on a routine basis.

Ask your friends what exercises they have found particularly helpful. Almost everyone knows some stretching movement that has worked to unkink a tricky trouble spot, to tighten a pocket of flab that made her dresses bulge in the wrong direction, or to improve circulation. Do remember, however, to breathe as rhythmically as you can while you exercise; never exercise if it hurts; and if you have a back or heart problem, consult your doctor first.

4. Positive Communication Exchange

It's been said that no man is an island. Well, no woman is an island either. None of us can live entirely alone. We need other people for many things—from companionship to help in emergencies.

It is very important to surround yourself with people who feel good about themselves, and who want to spread that goodness around. This is what is meant by PCE. It is necessary to get a little PCE each day. And to spread it around yourself. As your physical body becomes what you eat, so your mental being is what you think and what you hear and what you say. Think about what you have been hearing lately, what you have been saying.

Some people who are depressed and have a negative view of the world attempt to pass on that view (usually unconsciously, but misery *does* love company). At times depression can be contagious. Perhaps, for instance, you wake up feeling fine and are looking forward to your job when you leave your apartment. Then you run into your pessimistic, dour-faced neighbor, who greets you with "Didn't you sleep well? You're looking so run-down lately, dear. What's the matter, been sick again?"

Even if you were feeling fine just two seconds before, you may wonder, "What's the matter with me? Maybe I didn't get a good night's sleep." Then you begin to feel that ache in the back again, your feet drag a little, and by the time you get to work you feel that you're going to need three more cups of coffee just to make it to lunch.

Think for a moment about your social network—your lover, friends, family, neighbors, co-workers, and acquaintances. Are they usually supportive and optimistic? Do you look forward to being with them, or do they too often drag you down?

Your body and the energy that surrounds you can act like a magnet—collecting either positive or negative thoughts from the people near you, as you in turn affect them. The stronger and more positive your attitude, the more you will attract others. While it isn't always easy to get your energy level up, it helps to have some positively motivated individuals in your group and to repeat phrases like: "I feel fine," "My day is going very well," "I am handling things just right."

If your circle doesn't include enough optimistic, upbeat adults in it, seriously consider finding new friends and acquaintances by exploring your local women's center and attending lectures or discussion groups sponsored by a nearby YWCA, health center, library, college, religious group, or community center. You can also meet other women through work-related professional associations, seminars, or conferences. You might even want to experiment with an inexpensive weekend or evening adult class in one of your areas of interest. (For tips on meeting new and interesting men, turn to Chapter 11.)

5. Play Time

Everyone, from the very young to the very old, needs some play time. The name of the game may change, but the basic idea is the same. Play—whether hopscotch for children or cards, movies, dancing, parties, or bowling for adults—is having a good time, escaping from "the real world" for a little while. For adults, play serves some of the same purposes that it does for children: It is fun; it gives us a chance to expand ourselves, to explore and use our imaginations, and to fantasize a bit within safe boundaries. Play gives us real physical relief as well. Tensions melt away in laughter; the day's hassles, if they don't disappear entirely, are at least put into perspective and made a manageable size again.

The range of play experiences is endless. Depending on your personality and your environment, play could be making music on a harmonica, entering a game of volleyball, planning a weekly trip to the shore, visiting a singles bar, making pottery, exploring yard sales, or belly dancing. Women today, alone or with friends, have fun doing everything from playing pool to mountain climbing.

If you haven't found a play activity that really gives you pleasure, gets your body moving and your mind away from bills and bottles every now and then, perhaps you need to extend your circle or your interests. Life is just too short to spend going grimly through the same daily routine. No matter what your personal interests are, find people to share some fun with you. Whatever you do, make sure it:

- Gives you pleasure and some laughter;
- Gets your mind off work and children;
- Relieves some body tensions.

6. Safe Anger Outlet

The more you begin to treat yourself like a VIP, the better you are going to feel. Your body will respond to the tender loving care you'll be giving it and you'll be thinking more clearly and efficiently than ever. You may end up finding life 10 percent or 200 percent more manageable.

Unfortunately, however, there are still going to be days when life comes up with a few extra hard knocks on the chin. It happens to the best of planners, no matter how we may try to avoid it. Unjust as it may be, we don't always get what we deserve in life.

Physical activity on a regular basis—jogging, dance, calisthenics—can help discharge tension on ordinary days, but even these will not suffice on the really bad ones. Take Helen Vicardi. One day, minor aggravations and annoyances grew into a towering mountain of frustration by evening, and Helen was in serious need of a safe anger outlet.

"Before I left for my morning shift at the hospital I got another threatening letter in the mail. It was from this department store, saying if I didn't make immediate payment they were going to turn the bill over to a collection agency. I'd already made three calls to them to tell them I'd paid off that account two months ago. But their computer kept screwing up and it just wasn't recording my payment.

"I didn't have time to call them again and argue, so I kept on going to the bus stop. Just as I got to the stop I could see the bus had come early; it was already a block away. That meant I'd be late for work and annoy the nurse I was replacing. Not to mention it was freezing—by the time the next bus came my toes and fingers were like ice cubes."

Helen's whole day was a series of additional annoyances, including a surly doctor and a rude, obnoxious patient who wanted everything in the world. Each annoyance added to the next until by the end of her shift Helen's pulse was racing, her stomach knotted, and her neck rigid with accumulated angers.

"Just two blocks from home, this creep—this scum, really!—drove by real slow and said—I can't even repeat what he said. I mean this guy must have crawled out of a sewer. And you know how when things are on your mind it doesn't always register? By the time I realized he was talking to me, and what he'd said, he was three blocks up the street."

Helen's fury was at its peak when she walked into her apartment. And when one of her eight-year-old twins said, "Mom, you forgot the potato chips!" Helen had all she could do not to throw the bag of groceries she had just lugged up three flights of stairs.

What could she do? There was no way to yell at the faceless computer in the department store; it was impossible to confront the bus driver who had made her late for work, the obnoxious patient, or the obscene man in the car.

Helen wisely locked herself in her bedroom and beat on her pillows for a few minutes. It didn't hurt the pillows or her hands. And more important, it didn't hurt her son—who was the most likely candidate at that point for an angry discharge. When she came out of her room Helen had released enough pent-up anger to calmly explain to her twins that the day had been less than ideal.

Pillow punching is one example of a Safe Anger Outlet. But there are many other ways to handle dangerous overloads. Some women have found that it helps to run in place for several minutes until tiredness replaces anger. Others do pushups, literally beat a rug, kick around a soccer ball, or even give a punching bag a good workout. The idea is to release muscle tension, to get rid of excess adrenaline, to get anger out safely. Without some physical outlet it is all too easy for someone to get hurt, either you, your children, or a pet who hasn't the faintest idea of what s/he did wrong.

Anger held in can turn into a solid case of depression or can accumulate in little pockets of your body and create migraines, backaches, or stomach upsets. By then, you have totally forgotten what it was that set up the negative feelings in the first place.

If you decide to try the pillow punching technique, here are some things to remember:

- Set a time limit, say two to five minutes at first. That will speed up the process, and with your busy schedule you don't have time to hang on to angers that can only hold you back and make you miserable. Setting a time limit for getting anger out will also create safe boundaries within which you can work.

- Make sure those around you are not going to be frightened, inconvenienced, or endangered. Choose a private place, preferably your own room. If you want to scream it out, try screaming into pillows so your neighbors won't be wondering whether to call the police.

More important, if your children are around, explain to them what you are going to do, and make sure they understand that they are not the cause of your anger. While still young, children assume that the entire world revolves around them, that they are the cause of all things—especially those things they feel are negative in some way. This is why, whether children say so or not, they are often afraid they are to blame for Daddy's leaving or Mommy's headache. It is important to explain to them that you are not mad at them. Explain that it is normal—even though it may appear scary—to get angry from time to time. Also explain what it is you are angry about and that you don't want to hurt anyone so you are going to pretend the pillow is the bad guy. Ask for a few minutes alone and afterward reassure them that you love them. After the anger is gone, it will be easier to express the affection they need from you.

- Go to wherever you have chosen for privacy and say, "I am angry at . . ." and list whatever it is that has upset you.
- Picture the cause of your anger clearly and punch those problems out (with as much physical energy as you can put into it).
- Then imagine yourself strongly and efficiently dealing with those problems, and zapping them out of your world. Feel the negative energy flowing out of you, harmlessly, into space.
- See yourself becoming calmer. And say something positive to yourself about dealing with the problem and not letting it continue to bother you: "That is behind me. It can't affect me anymore."
- Give your kids a hug, and enjoy the good feelings that will come with the release of all that tension.

Here are other outlets that you might want to explore:

- Take a self-defense course—one that includes a lot of body movement, like the martial arts of aikido or kung fu, or even basic street-defense courses now offered at many YWCAs or women's centers. These arts add confidence, increased self-esteem, better coordination, grace, and fitness, as well as providing excellent stress outlets. Consider enrolling daughters or young sons, especially if you are living in or near a high-crime area.

- Try swimming, one of the best all-round exercises available. Your local YWCA, community center, or municipal pool might be the solution to routine stress reduction.

- Organize a women's bowling or volleyball team (or softball in the summer) if you have access to an empty school gymnasium. These can be great social gatherings and a chance for a night out as well.

- Dance whenever and wherever possible. Even a quick five or ten minutes of lively movement in your kitchen or living room can make a big difference.

However you do it, whatever your personal preference, start developing a routine tension outlet. Without it, those migraines or stomach problems may be around for much too long.

7. Love Sessions

No VIP's week would be complete without some reward for long days, patience, and continued growth, some special reminder that all work and no time out makes Jill a dull girl, and an unhealthy one. You may say, "Yes, I care about myself." But how are you showing it? One way is with a weekly or twice weekly Love Session.

Some VIPs can afford to take advantage of health spas to unwind, with some form of water therapy and hour-long massages. If you can afford a trip to a spa or health center, consider treating yourself on some special occasion to see if you might enjoy the experience on a regular basis.

While full-scale health spas with organized programs and professional staffs tend to be costly, saunas, whirlpools, hot tubs, and steam baths are now available for do-it-yourselfers at many public pools. In some areas, swimming pools and water-therapy facilities are offered on a daily fee or a package-plan basis at hotels. Depending on where you live, you may even be able to install a hot tub or sauna on your own property at moderate cost.

Even with an ordinary tub or shower, your own home can easily become your private health center. If you have young children, wait until they're in bed so they don't interrupt your special hour with requests for cookies and milk. If your children are older, let them know that while they are doing their homework or watching television, the bathroom is going to be your turf, for at least one uninterrupted hour.

If you have been crashing through the week taking two-minute showers, now is the time to stop and let water do its magic. Soaking in a warm tub is a natural healing tool. It is also, for many women, one way to say "I love my body." Make the experience as luxurious as you can:

- Have your best and softest towels handy.
- If you have a bright overhead light, use a candle to create a more relaxing mood.
- Try fragrant soaps like lavender, rose, or aloe vera (a green soap made from the aloe plant which has a soothing effect on many types of skin; glycerine soaps might be better if your skin is oily).
- Experiment with a new shampoo, conditioner, or facial.
- If your skin is dry, add some oils to the water; olive or safflower will do in a pinch.
- Pick something wonderful to get into after your bath. If you don't have a robe or nightgown that makes you feel movie-star elegant, add one to your list of treats for the future.

Once in the tub, find a comfortable position and lie back. For a few minutes just let the water carry your weight; let your head relax totally in the water, and breathe deeply in and out. Feel the water loosening the knots, all the way from your neck to your toes.

Once you begin to feel calmer, slowly massage your face: those areas of high tension around the hairline, between the eyes—especially if you tent to squint—around your jaw and mouth. Move your fingers in small circles, very gently all over your face, more deeply to reach any particularly tight areas. Working toward your toes, slowly lather up your entire body. Massage those areas where you have been carrying the most body tension (often in the calves, shoulders, lower back). And don't neglect your hands and feet! Thousands of nerve endings are concentrated in your overworked extremities. Foot massage, working up a good lather and exerting more pressure on the soles, can feel amazingly good.

Finish up your bath with a one- or two-minute shower and then apply lotion to dry spots—elbows, hands, heels, knees— treating yourself with the same tenderness you would a loved one.

If you have tension spots that no amount of soaking can loosen up, massage—either by yourself or with a good friend—can't be recommended too highly. Unfortunately, "massage parlors" that function mainly as connections for quick sexual encounters have given massage a bad press. But massage has been used as a healing art in many cultures for thousands of years. It can be used to restore circulation after your foot falls asleep or to relieve a headache caused by tention. Massage is a good alternative to prescription muscle relaxants; it is safer than tranquilizers and has no druggy side effects.

If you can afford an occasional VIP personal luxury (fifteen or twenty dollars is now the standard fee), you might seek out a professional massager through a women's center, spa, or YWCA. If you are interested in learning some massage techniques and practicing with a friend, an excellent introductory book for beginners is recommended at the end of this chapter.

8. Consciousness Cleansing
Rather than ending your day with a violent shoot-'em-up, or poring over a pile of bills, try a five- to fifteen-minute Consciousness Cleansing. Now is the time to relax your mind and body in preparation for sleep. Sit quietly, as with your QMT, to clear your head of all the day's white noise. Then lie down, stretch out, and tune in some soothing music. The last part of each day you should be on relaxed automatic pilot, and looking forward to pleasant dreams.

9. Sleep

Are you getting enough? Sleep is your basic healing time, when your body will do its own renewing, if you let it. Some single mothers are always more than ready for bed and have no difficulty going out like a light. But for others, the stresses are so extreme that it takes a long time to unwind. If you have problems getting to sleep, wake in the middle of the night, or do sleep but don't feel refreshed by it, try one or more of the following:

• Begin early in the evening to wind down family activities: Get all the day's negative happenings (fights at school, homework hassles, etc.) cleared away early on; if you have to, set a time line for discussion, debate, and problem solving.

• Try an herbal, non-caffeinated tea instead of coffee after dinner or just before bed. Breathe in a little of the steam before sipping a cup of peppermint, chamomile, or some herbal mix of your own soothing favorites.

• Put on your most relaxing records (especially music without lyrics) or tune in a soft-music station, low volume, by your bed. Drift with it, shut your eyes, and don't worry if it stays on all night.

• Invest in a record of natural sounds—wind in the trees, ocean waves, light rain on a roof.

• Read a good novel (not *The Walking Dead* or *Killer Vampire*) in bed or on the couch; being horizontal is often being halfway to sleep.

• Make up a good fantasy (romantic or not), especially one with lots of detail in it. Some women find themselves trailing off to sleep in the middle of "scene setting."

Source notes
1. E. Greywolf, M. Reese, and D. Belle, "Stressed Mothers Syndrome," *Behavioral Medicine,* November 1980.

References

The Boston Women's Health Book Collective. *Our Bodies, Ourselves,** New York: Simon & Schuster, 1979.

The Diagram Group. *The Healthy Body: A Maintenance Manual.* New York: New American Library, 1981.

Downing, George. *The Massage Book.* New York: Random House, 1972.

Lettvin, Maggie. *Maggie's Woman's Book.** Boston: Houghton Mifflin, 1980.

Miller, Don. *Bodymind: The Whole Person Health Book.* Englewood Cliffs, N.J.: Prentice-Hall, 1974.

* Especially recommended

CHAPTER FIVE

Making Sense of Nutrition

You see so many contradictory articles on nutrition it gets confusing. I think schools should offer parents classes. I'd really like to get some straight answers.

Today consumers are bombarded with seemingly endless nutritional advice from articles and advertisements. This information is often difficult to digest not only because it is filled with technical jargon but also because it is contradictory. For example, many nutritional experts, like Dr. David Ruben, are extremely concerned about chemical additives in our food and advocate what would amount to a complete revamping of the average American diet. Other experts disagree, claiming that synthetic additives are a necessary and harmless part of the food chain, and that the average American diet is fairly healthy.

Yet as the person who decides what food goes on the family table, you must make sense out of all this, because we literally are what we eat, becoming new people about every seven years as old cells die and new ones take their places.

There are six major reasons why it is important to be a selective food consumer. Wholesome meals can:

- Supply your family's basic health needs and decrease the number of visits you will make to the doctor or dentist;
- Affect your own and your child's behavior;
- Improve physical appearance;
- Prolong life;
- Give you more control (and the food industry less) over your life;
- Save you money.

But how can we be sure which items we should be adding to our grocery list, and which we should be avoiding?

A LOOK AT THE EXPERTS

When considering your family's dietary needs, it is wise to consider the source of all the information you receive. Some influential organizations sound official, like the Food and Nutrition Board of the National Academy of Sciences-National Research Council (NAS-NRC). This group puts out information on the RDA (recommended daily allowances) for vitamins and minerals. We see these on the labels of the foods and pills we buy, and often trust that these recommendations offer us accurate guidelines. But what is this organization?

David Ruben advises us that the NAS-NRC is not a government agency. Nor is it related to a university, research center, or consumer group. It is, Ruben says, "just a nifty little private business organized and owned by food manufacturers and vitamin sellers."[1] Ruben believes the Food and Nutrition Board influences our federal Food and Drug Administration (FDA), which also has its list of RDAs, and points out that the board's recommended allowances of vitamins and minerals are sometimes up to 250 percent more than recommendations by the nonprofit World Health Organization.

Some organizations that appear to be consumer groups have

ties to private food processers. According to consumer reporter Marian Burros, Consumer Alert—which sounds as if it should be on the side of concerned citizens—actually gets its money from "chemical companies and the soft drink trade associations."[2]

Even more alarming, Burros cites companies and trade associations that offer schools "reams of free material that parades as nutrition information . . . [such as] 'Cooking with Dr. Pepper' [which] features the history of soft drinks, nutritional information about the product . . . plus about 40 recipes. And you wondered why your child wants to make corn bread with a package of cornbread mix and a bottle of Dr. Pepper!"[3]

Even following the advice of official government spokespersons does not assure food safety. Food producers and chemical companies maintain powerful lobbies that influence government decisions. Time after time, the FDA has approved additives, such as artificial food dyes, nitrites, and saccharine, which have ultimately proved harmful. One startling example is DES (diethylstilbestrol), used to stimulate growth in cattle—until it was found to cause vaginal cancer and testicular abnormalities in the babies of women who took this drug during pregnancy. The drug was not banned for use until 1979.[4]

The simple fact is that much remains to be learned about the more than five thousand chemicals now being used by food processors. Even though some chemicals may not be harmful in small doses, or by themselves, no one really knows what the long-range effects are of mixing hundreds, or thousands, of different synthetic chemicals in the body. Using these chemicals simplifies things for food producers (allowing longer storage, enhancing appearance, and improving other qualities of foods) but it doesn't simplify the process of preparing healthy meals for your family. For the time being, it seems wisest to avoid foods containing artificial chemicals whenever possible.

THE TRUTH ABOUT ADVERTISERS

Most of our information about food comes from TV commercials and printed advertisements, which often stretch very, very thin the truth-in-advertising laws.

Rodger Doyle and James Redding, two professors of consumerism and nutrition, compared advertising expenditures with nutritional value for the one hundred most heavily promoted food brands. Only seven of the one hundred received an "A"—indicating the food contained substantial nutrients and had few questionable ingredients or additives. (Ninety-eight had at least one additive.) Thirty-seven flunked the test "because they contained no nutrients other than calories!"[5]

What about "enriched" and "fortified" foods? Despite the ads, these artificial enrichments do not replace what is lost from foods in processing. Many white breads, for example, are stripped of about twenty-five nutrients and of natural fiber, and then only half a dozen or so vitamins and/or minerals (often the cheapest rather than the most important) are put back in.

IS THERE A FORMULA?

Because nutrition is not an exact science, and no two individuals are physically identical, it is impossible to give an exact formula for the best of all possible diets. But analysis of the average American diet does pinpoint imbalances which contribute to some of our major health problems, such as obesity, heart disease, cancer, and diabetes. In general, it is likely that your family could greatly benefit from a reduction of:

- Sugar
- Salt
- Refined grains
- Fats and oils

- Chemical additives (food dyes, retardants which slow spoilage, flavor enhancers, bleaches, clarifying agents, and other chemicals which soften, thicken, neutralize, dry out, or artificially moisten foods and alter them in some way)
- Caffeine (found not only in coffee and tea but in chocolate, soft drinks, and diet colas). Colas, incidentally, have the equivalent of eight teaspoons of sugar per twelve-ounce container, as well as the highest acidity of all soft drinks. They are real tooth-decay promoters.[6]

These items are found in enormous quantities in most of the processed foods we find in the supermarket. It has been estimated that we consume annually up to one hundred thirty pounds of sugars, at least ten times the amount of salt we really need, and between five and six pounds of synthetic chemical additives. Most of us could benefit from replacing some quantity of these items with:

- Fresh fruits, *small* amounts of honey, or the chocolate substitute, carob;
- Whole grains (whole wheat, rye, millet);
- Polyunsaturated vegetable oils;
- Fresh foods that don't contain high quantities of additives;
- A variety of beverage alternatives such as herbal teas, fruit and vegetable juices, or spring water.

THE SUGAR MONSTER

As most mothers know, supermarkets appear to have been designed and stocked by a sugar monster. And if he doesn't get you with the lanes of sugared cereals, sodas, and snack foods, he'll grab your child's attention with candies while you are hemmed in line just before the cash register.

Avoiding the obvious sources—candies, pastries, ice cream, and other goodies—does not solve the problem because sugar is the largest component in many cereals, and is consistently overused in fruit juices, canned and frozen fruits and vegetables, mayonnaise, salad dressing, canned and frozen prepared dishes, cheese spreads, mixes, and thousands of other items. Sugar is cheap and also relatively heavy. For goods priced by weight, it makes an inexpensive additive. It is useful, too, for adding bulk to soups, gravy, and ketchup, and for making the bland flavor of highly processed foods more palatable.

An overabundance of sugar has been linked not only to tooth decay and gum diseases but to obesity, diabetes, and hypoglycemia. Some studies indicate that it may also be related to hyperactivity in children.

To calculate the amount of hidden and other sugar your family consumes, write down everything that goes into your mouth and your child's for one day. The following day check off each food that contained sugar. In addition to figuring every teaspoon of sugar you added to coffee, tea, or desserts, take a good look at the labels on cans, frozen goods, and mixes you used in preparing meals. The ingredients on labels are supposed to be listed in order of quantity. Packaged foods with sugar among the first few ingredients (often listed as dextrose, corn syrup, lactose, sucrose) are therefore those with the highest sugar content. In Doyle and Redding's check of the one hundred most heavily advertised food products, seventy-seven had sugar as the first or second ingredient.

Giving up a large portion of the two or more pounds of sugar you are probably eating every week would be a healthy thing to do. But even a 10 percent reduction in the amount of sugar your family consumes is a big step in the right direction.

While you are cutting out sugar, you will probably be eliminating salt as well; often the same foods that have been bulked with sugar and other additives are also oversalted. Highly salted foods can also be avoided by checking labels and by weaning your children away from potato chips and other packaged snacks to the more wholesome ones listed below. Adding tasty herbs and spices to the dishes you prepare from scratch will allow you to cut down on yet more salt and sugar.

THE STAFF OF LIFE

With the invention of steel-roller milling, two of the natural components of a grain of wheat (the bran and the wheat germ) were removed, along with most of the wheat's protein, vitamins, and minerals. What is left is a starchy endosperm, essentially empty calories. To this refined wheat are added numerous chemicals that keep flour products long-lasting but questionably doctored. The "enrichments" added to some flour products are never enough to repair the damage done by the milling. Reducing the amount of refined flour products—white bread, rolls and buns, pancakes, muffins, pasta—your family eats is a wise consumer step to take. And you can do this without a sudden, drastic change in meal planning.

• Alternate white-bread sandwiches and dinner rolls with products made from stone-ground whole wheat, rye, oatmeal, and other grains. Experiment until you find a few brands your family really enjoys. Or try baking your own—few children can resist fresh-out-of-the-oven bread.

• Include some whole-wheat, soy, or other flour in recipes calling for all-white. Experiment until you find the best proportions, starting with one fifth to one quarter of the amount called for in your recipes. Sometimes you can substitute whole-wheat flour entirely, as in coatings for chicken and other meats (in place of expensive, chemicalized packets of instant coating mix).

• Buy whole-wheat linguini, egg noodles, macaroni, or other pasta, or try the new soy versions (which have much more protein), and introduce them gradually by combining them with white-flour pastas or adding them to homemade soups.

SPEAKING OF FAT

The average American diet consists of 42 percent fat, much more than is needed for a healthy nutritional balance. It is little wonder that the majority of us periodically undertake one form of diet or another. We consume too much fat (and oil) and the wrong kinds—the saturated varieties. Saturated fats and oils are those that cannot easily be broken down by the body. (Most fats of animal origin, including milk and dairy products, bacon drippings, lard, and chicken fat, contain saturated fats.) They can clog arteries, affect the heart, and cause other kinds of health problems, aside from storing themselves uselessly in our bodies and making it harder for us to zip up our clothes. Liquid oils of vegetable origin are usually polyunsaturated (though some exceptions are listed below) and should make up the bulk of your fat consumption.

While you would not want to cut out fats entirely, or give up an occasional splurge of sour cream on a baked potato or in a sauce, here are ways to reduce your saturated fat consumption yet still dine in style.

- Replace the butter on your potatoes and other vegetables with low-fat cheddar or cottage cheese, or with a polyunsaturated margarine.
- Mix up your own salad dressing (approximately half vinegar and half vegetable oil with a lot of herbs and garlic to taste) for a healthier, more tasty dressing than the bottled, chemicalized versions—at a fraction of the cost.
- Use dried milk instead of whole milk for your cooking needs. Enough dried milk can be mixed up to meet your immediate needs and the remainder stored for a long time. It is much less expensive, and in most recipes it cannot be detected as a whole-milk substitute.
- Cut down on your intake of fatty meats—a major source of the fats you ingest in your daily meals.
- Check the labels on all products you buy to see whether they contain saturated fats and oils. The labels may say saturated, hydrogenated, hardened, partially saturated, or partially hydrogenated, or they may list the type of oil. *Unsaturated* oils are corn, cottonseed, safflower, sesame, soybean, sunflower seed, and walnut oil. Avóid palm, peanut, rice, and coconut oils as well as

cocoa butter, all of which are highly saturated. These oils are often used in making imitation dairy products (whips, imitation cream and ice cream, and some imitation cheeses) and bakery goods. Olive, avocado, and some nut oils fall between these two extremes.

PROTEIN: THE GREAT MEAT MYTH

We all need protein that contains the collection of amino acids that our bodies can't manufacture by themselves. But cheaper, healthier, less fattening, and more efficient protein sources than meat are available.

Meats such as beef and pork contain very high quantities of saturated fat in relation to the amount of available protein. Most families could easily reduce the amount of meat they eat and achieve beneficial side effects. Even the basics, like burgers and lasagna, can be turned into less fat and more protein by eliminating half the beef in favor of a substitute made of soybeans (in granular form it mixes with eggs and water like hamburger). If you use half and half, it's unlikely your child will even notice the difference, especially if it's topped with melted cheese.

Eliminating meat entirely would not be harmful (as the nearly one billion vegetarians of the world prove) as long as you substitute another source of protein. The main traditional substitutes for meat are eggs, dairy products, and fish, but proper combinations of grains and vegetables also provide inexpensive protein. For the mother concerned with obesity, health, and cutting the food budget, Frances Lappe (*Diet for a Small Planet*) and Ellen Buchman Ewald (*Recipes for a Small Planet*) provide all the necessary information and hundreds of delicious recipes.

With imaginative combinations based on brown rice and other whole grains, nuts, dairy products, and a variety of beans and other vegetables, your family can dine deliciously on Mexican, Greek, Oriental, and other ethnic delicacies, as well as some great American favorites. For more exotic and fast meals (thirty minutes or under), check out a copy of Marion Burros's *Keep it Simple.*

ONE STEP AT A TIME

Even if you want to change your diet, you can't hope to correct years of poor eating habits overnight. Trying to wean your child suddenly from colas, chocolate cupcakes, and dyed cheese twists to whole-wheat bean-sprout sandwiches could be as traumatic for you as trying to take a fresh bone away from a dog.

Changes in diet should be made one step at a time. You might start with tasty substitutes for snacks and desserts that most children are guaranteed to like. Be on the lookout for simple but wholesome recipes that your children can prepare themselves, or with minimal help from you. The following suggestions provide many times the nutritional value of most processed snacks or sweets, without the chemicals and exorbitant amounts of sugar and salt. You or your child can prepare them with minimal effort, and at far less cost than similar snacks found on your market shelves.

- Your own special version of campers' "gorp" can be easily put together with raisins and bits of other dried fruits, nuts, sunflower seeds, and a sprinkling of chocolate morsels.
- Homemade granola, peanut butter, or oatmeal-and-raisin cookies are just as appealing as store-boughts (see recipe books suggested at the end of this chapter). And collect recipes for foods that can be made in a batch and frozen, or for doughs or other mixtures that can be thawed and/or baked a bit at a time.
- Granola is another snack children can easily make at home. It can also be eaten as a substitute for sugar-laden breakfast cereals when mixed with sliced fruits and milk or fresh-fruit yogurts.
- Popcorn is a cheap treat if you pop it yourself (you can do so in minutes) and add a little unsaturated margarine and less salt than in the bought variety. Some families save money by preparing it ahead and taking small, individually wrapped bags to the movies.

- If your child is unwilling to eat a piece of fruit for a dessert or snack, start off by introducing tempting combinations like bananas and orange slices topped with a bit of coconut.

- Cubes of natural, unsweetened fruit juice are simple to freeze in an ice-cube tray or Popsicle mold and cost a fraction of what Popsicles do in shops. This one-step goody can easily become "slush" for cones just by leaving out the ice cube divider and removing the juice before it becomes completely frozen.

- Frozen-fruit yogurt cubes can be made the same way and are much less expensive than store-boughts, especially if you buy plain or vanilla yogurt and add your own fruit. The fresh-fruit varieties are a bit more expensive but come in luscious flavors.

- Instead of expensive, yellow-dyed cheese snacks, layer whole-wheat toast with a favorite cheese, brown in the oven, then cut in bit-sized squares.

- Delicious, inexpensive milk shakes are quickly made in a blender (or with electric beaters) by combining a cup of milk or two, some banana, yogurt, vanilla—the real kind, not the artificial "vanillin"—and a bit of nutmeg and cinnamon, or by using berries or other fruit with or without complementary spices.

- Individual snack pizzas can be made with whole-wheat English muffins or pita bread and a few slices of tomato, cheese, paprika, basil, and whatever other herbs you want to add.

WEIGHING THE COST

A large number of the processed foods sold today provide little but empty calories. Fruits and vegetables lose nutrients at a rapid rate when they are heated, treated, frozen, canned, or bottled. David Ruben traces the fresh garden pea on its journey to your supermarket: Thirty percent of its vitamins are lost at the canning plant simply from cooking; 25 percent are lost in sterilization; 27 percent end up in the discarded liquid; 12 percent of the remaining nutrients are lost when you heat the canned product after opening. Whatever you pay for a canned pea, you are getting only about 6 percent of its original nutrient value.

To get the most in fruits and vegetables for your food dollar, keep in mind:

- Foods grown in your own garden offer the best health value (assuming the soil is not depleted and foods are not heavily sprayed with pesticides)
- Next best offerings are fresh foods from the market.
- Frozen foods have fewer nutrients left in them.
- Canned foods have least of all.
- Try to include some fresh, uncooked fruits and vegetables in your meals each week (and wash them thoroughly, but don't soak, to eliminate any chemical residues).
- When cooking these foods, use as little water as possible; use a steamer rather than putting foods directly in water.
- Vitamins and minerals are found in or directly under the skins of many foods. You discard useful nutrients when you throw away the peelings.
- Cover your pans and use low heat rather than high; try cooking your vegetables a few minutes fewer than you normally do—this leaves them with a firmer texture and more natural goodness.
- Use cut-up foods as soon as possible and be sure to wrap and refrigerate immediately those foods you don't use right away. Leaving foods at room temperature destroys nutrients rapidly.

GOOD INVESTMENTS

Delicious meals, in addition to providing nutrition, are a celebration of life. They not only give sensual satisfaction; when lovingly prepared and shared with others, they provide creative satisfaction as well. When viewed as an art, cooking can be fun, an exciting step in self-expression for children as well as parents. With practice, some imagination, and a sense of experimentation, the kitchen can become a satisfying family room.

Many women enjoy gardening, and even in the city they can satisfy their green thumbs with urban "mini-gardens" in containers on terraces or rooftops, or even in windowboxes. If you have a porch that gets some sun, you are that much further ahead, and some women get exercise as well by joining community gardens where they can have their own vegetable plots. Even if you do not want to go in for fruit and vegetable gardening, many herbs—basil, chives, thyme, and dozens more— are beautiful, fragrant, and easy to grow indoors or outdoors. Young plants can be picked up in many supermarkets, florist shops, and gardening centers, and are then available to add to the cooking pot.

Experimenting with a new herb or spice each week or so can add tremendous interest to your foods, eliminating the need for excess salt or sugar. Fresh herbs are obviously better than the dried varieties, and your child will feel extra pampered if you brew a few leaves of home-grown peppermint to soothe an upset stomach.

Other excellent investments for smart consumers are:

Food processors or blenders. These can pay for themselves very quickly and come in handy for preparing milk shakes, sauces, bread crumbs, fruit drinks, pureed vegetables for soups, or even baby foods (just put in potatoes, carrots or other cooked vegetables, fruit, or the meat you are preparing for your own dinner, and mix with a little water). Making your own baby foods is not much more effort than buying expensive canned ones, and of course, it eliminates the unnecessary salt, sugar, and other questionable ingredients you may find in processed infant foods.

A slow-cooking electric pot. Slow cookers, safely used, can save you many hours of frantic, last-minute dinner preparation, as well as transforming cheap, tough cuts of meat into tender, fall-apart delights.

A good, sharp set of knives. Cheap, blunt knives that don't hold an edge are a hazard to any cook. They also cut jagged, raggedy edges in vegetables, meat and fruit—leaving extra surfaces exposed to air and nutrient loss before and during cooking.

A meat thermometer. This item helps you avoid ruining more expensive cuts of meat and assures that roasts come out exactly as you want them.

Steamers. These are collapsible wire "baskets" that fit inside your pans and keep vegetables and fruits out of water while they cook.

Cookie cutters. With these you and your child together can share memorable and fun hours, especially if the cookie dough is mixed with a lot of love and some good old-fashioned, healthy ingredients like honey, whole wheat, nuts, and fruits.

Source Notes
1. David Ruben, *Everything You Always Wanted to Know About Nutrition* (New York: Simon & Schuster, 1978), p. 90.
2. Marian Burros, *Keep It Simple* (New York: Pocket Books, 1981), p. 38.
3. Ibid., p. 31.
4. Ibid., p. 35.
5. Rodger Doyle and James Redding, *The Complete Food Handbook* (New York: Grove Press, 1976), p. 5.
6. Ibid., p. 239.
7. Ibid., p. 5.
8. Ruben, op. cit., p. 77.
9. Ibid., p. 155.
10. Doyle and Redding, op. cit., p. 25.

References
Bernarde, Melvin. *The Chemicals We Eat.* New York: McGraw-Hill, 1971.
Burros, Marian. *Keep It Simple.** New York: Pocket Books, 1981.
Doyle, Rodger, and James Redding. *The Complete Food Handbook.** New York: Grove Press, 1976.
Ewald, Ellen Buchman. *Recipes for a Small Planet.** New York: Ballantine, 1973.
Lappe, Frances Moore. *Diet for a Small Planet.** New York: Ballantine, 1971.
Miller, Don. *Bodymind: The Whole Person Health Book.* Englewood Cliffs, N.J.: Prentice-Hall, 1974.
Ruben, David. *Everything You Always Wanted to Know About Nutrition.* New York: Simon & Schuster, 1978.

* Highly recommended

CHAPTER SIX

Pioneering:
New Pathways
to the Future

I'm not saying it's easy. But there are so many more opportunities than when my mother was growing up. In a way, we are pioneers.

The speed at which the world around us is changing has greatly accelerated during the twentieth century, especially since World War II. This acceleration is most obvious to those who live in larger cities. As author Alvin Toffler has pointed out in *Future Shock,* there is an almost science-fictionlike shifting of the landscape in which city dwellers live. Entire neighborhoods are demolished and new, more modern structures rise in no time at all. Cars, buildings, and roadways are continually redesigned. Even the smallest items of consumption are changing. Everything from toothpaste tubes to safety pins is frequently reconstructed and repackaged.

These day-to-day changes accelerate us into the future at such a rate that even one generation past can seem very alien to us. Imagine, for example, the 1940s when many married couples were separated by war and a large percentage of the world's people were still farming for a living. It was a world before television and computers, where middle America sat on front porches reading the *Saturday Evening Post,* and young lovers walked to the local theater to see movies like *Gone with the Wind.*

The differences from the world of our grandparents seem even more amazing—almost ancient history. At the turn of the century the family car was still the family horse, and people hauled in blocks of ice to keep their food from spoiling. Popping a package of frozen buns into a microwave oven would have appeared magical. And women's work in the home was endless. Mothers made their children's clothes (and practically everything else) by hand. Cooking for a large family was an all-day chore, and "free time" meant mending, crocheting, or making doilies for "the front parlor."

Sexuality, of course, was rarely discussed openly; intimacy remained a mystery to be solved by each woman individually. Women experienced the very real possibility of death in childbirth each time they conceived, and had to deal with the frustrations and fears resulting from the lack of any safe birth-control options.

DREAM GAPS

How can one, psychologically and emotionally, make sense of—and find security in—a world that is constantly shifting its legal, economic, political, and social faces? With the thousands of changes occurring every year, confusion and resistance to change are a part of each generation. But adaptation may be more difficult than ever before, especially for older individuals or those who must deal with many changes quickly.

New ideas are frequently harder to adjust to than changes in our physical world. Many of the material changes in the last generation can easily be fitted into our parents' dreams of how the world should be. Most people, for example, now take television for granted. It is a major source of communication, an acknowledged advance over the radio. Even older people, although they may object to the programming, use television daily. But ideas are another matter.

Some of us thrive on new ideas. Others find the gaps between new and old too wide to bridge easily. This is most obvious in such touchy subjects as religion, sexuality, or politics. Often clashes occur in these areas between the dreams of one generation and the dreams of another.

For single mothers, these gaps often take the form of family arguments and disruptions, of negative feedback from neighbors and society at large, or even from old friends who choose more traditional life-styles than those many single mothers are now living. Sometimes these gaps are easily overcome. At other times, there is difficulty in dealing with the present.

Then and Now

Many women feel life in their mothers' day was simpler, quieter, less filled with hassles of the kinds women are now meeting. As one woman said, "A married woman with kids had a certain respected, untouchable position. People, especially men, were polite and considerate (chauvinistic perhaps) to women then. Now men are generally unhelpful, competing for the same jobs, and often hostile and rude. I have to deal with all this as well as muggers, thieves, pimps, and just violent street people daily because of my income, because of living in a city, and because of the times."

Some women feel that generational differences are two-edged, sometimes positive and sometimes extremely challenging. These women are aware that the new opportunities they enjoy as single mothers come with added responsibilities. And at times the responsibilities can draw on all their resources. The joys of more freedom of movement within society (of, for example, "not having anybody tell me what to do") can sometimes turn to pain on trying days when one has no one else to lean on.

Some women, however, dwell mainly on the positive

changes that single parenting has brought them, those that liberate them from some of the constraints of the past. These women are leading life-styles their mothers never imagined were possible (and which, in fact, were not possible only a few decades ago). These women are pioneers in every sense of the word.

Three Women

The three women in this chapter share some of the common experiences of pioneering new lives for themselves and their children. In exploring new life possibilities, they have knocked up against the old values of their families, their neighbors, and friends, and their larger society. While sometimes these hard knocks have hurt, each woman feels a greater wholeness about herself today that has come from carving out new space as a single woman and as a single mother.

In order to do this, each woman has had to deal with the dream gaps that exist between past traditions and twentieth-century freedoms and responsibilities. Some of the old ways had to be laid aside, and new dreams created and carried out, before they could fit themselves into our changing times. Coping can sometimes be frightening, sometimes exhilarating.

Though some struggles are common to many single mothers, others are unique to individuals. Some of the experiences of these three women will therefore be familiar to you, while others will not.

The gaps that women experience between where they want to go and where they have been expected to go are not confined to any particular income, race, religion, or ethnic group. The three women in this chapter have very different backgrounds, for instance, and began their early adult lives with extremely different expectations of what was "normal." Janice Wheeler was raised in a wealthy, white Connecticut suburb; Jenny Jackson is a black woman who was born in a small town in Alabama; and Kathy MacDonald is the daughter of Irish immigrants living in Massachusetts.

How have these three women successfully handled the transitions in their lives? With the dream gaps and the challenges of single parenting, each has had, as the bottom line, to come to believe in herself, to trust her choices and live with the results of those choices as she makes a new life for herself and her family.

JANICE WHEELER

My mother was a kept woman.

Janice Wheeler lived, for a while, the American Dream. Reared in a well-to-do home, at twenty-one Janice married an insurance executive and moved into a new ninety-thousand-dollar house in a spacious Connecticut suburb. She had her own car, a pool, and a closet full of expensive clothes. Within five years, she had had two healthy children.

Today, at thirty-six, Janice is divorced and lives in a four-room apartment in an inner city. She has traded the financial security she once had for a nine-to-five job with a local publishing house. "I've been rich," Janice said, "and I've been poor. I wouldn't say that money is happiness, but it can make things much easier. Still, if I had to choose again, I'd choose the divorce."

Janice feels her parents' affluence, rather than giving her a head start, actually created many illusions which she had to learn to deal with before she could begin to create a new life. The values of her own generation clashed drastically at times with those of her parents.

"My mother and I just don't hold the same things sacred. My mother was always saying to me, 'Once you get married, it's forever.'

"I feel like I was raised in a complete fantasy world, in this showplace house. You grow up thinking wicked people get punished, but the world isn't just. Evil people don't always get punished; good people don't always come out on top. And if you work hard, you don't always make it. It took me a long time to get over the way I was raised to think. I was taught such different standards that in some ways I'm always at war with myself.

"Even simple things. My mother and grandmother would flip if they saw me drinking a can of beer. It's not socially accepted in my family. It's the good old martini. I don't like martinis.

"At one time I was trying to live their dream. I was following my mother's footsteps: decorating the house, doing the bridge club, doing the whole scene. I hated it, though I thought that's what life was all about. My mother was a kept woman. I doubt my mother will ever accept what I'm trying to do. But one thing I have learned: Women don't owe their whole lives to their families. It's really hard sometimes, being single, but now I feel like a whole person, not just somebody's less important half.

"I had to learn the hard way after the divorce. My ex moved out of state and has avoided paying me a cent. At first my parents took me and the kids in. But they constantly made remarks about what I was doing to the kids by divorcing their father, and how this would 'appear' to other people they knew.

"So I moved out and got an apartment. I had to go on welfare that first year while I was getting myself together and job hunting. But I thought I was handling things pretty well.

"But my parents didn't think so—and they let me know about it. The last straw was when they began to treat me and the kids like poor relatives. By being poor I had this lowly status and my children were not treated as well as my sister's children. So I stopped writing, calling, or visiting them, for over a year.

"I had to show them I wasn't a weak, dependent person. That I could take care of myself and not have to come for a drop of help if they were going to treat my kids that way. I'm not well-off—if you help me out a little it's a big help. But if you don't, I'm going to make it without you.

"When they realized I was serious, that I simply wasn't going to communicate with them again, that's when they began to change. I just wouldn't give in. Then they stopped getting on me about my life. And if anything, they began to overindulge the kids.

"Having to learn about money was one of the hardest things for me. When I had to go on welfare that first year, I used to get depressed all the time, blaming myself for everything. Every two weeks, when I got my check, I'd plan how to stretch it out. But I blew it every time. So I'd be in the same situation, thinking, 'What am I going to do?,' the last few days before the next check arrived. I used to try to figure out how to feed us. It was that basic.

"Not having a car, there was no place to go—so I was stuck sitting there thinking about it. I would sit on the porch with Pammy and Robbie and feel not only depressed but angry. Because the last few days before the check would come would be so bad and I'd tell myself, 'I'm not going to go crazy with this money fear; I'm going to try to make it last this time.'

"The constant go-round was incredibly upsetting. And it was worse when something unexpected came up. One day the washing machine broke. When I called a repairman he told me I had to pay cash. So I paid him out of the rent money, and then took the receipt to welfare. But they said they wouldn't pay for it because I hadn't followed the proper procedure.

"So here my rent was blown and I had to talk to my landlord and work out payments to catch up on my rent. It cut things so short for a few months it was ridiculous. I guess some good came out of it, though, because after that experience I bought a book on home repairs. Now if I have to call a repairman I stand and watch really closely, even if it bothers them. The next time I have the problem, I can usually fix it myself.

"Then there was another problem with the landlord. In the winter my kitchen would be roasting hot while my living room was freezing. When the pipes froze my landlord told me not to flush until spring. Can you believe it? For six months he was getting rent while I had no hot water, and I was trying to bring this man to court. It was very hard to live without hot water. I had just never experienced it.

"It was so unjust—even now I feel as though somebody owes me something. At the hearing, when he was asked, 'Do you provide hot water for this woman?,' the landlord said, 'Yes.' And I had cold, ice-cold water in my apartment. I got to the point where I wanted to get up and jump on that man it was so frustrating. In the end I had to move and I felt so powerless.

"It was hard on me, but I really worried about the kids. My son, Robbie, who was nine, couldn't stand it all. After two years he began having emotional problems and asked if he could move in with his grandparents. The land of milk and plenty, you know. I tried to change his mind for several months but then decided it was wrong to try to force him to stay with me. He's been living with them for a year now.

"It put a terrible strain on Pammy too. Once—it is sort of funny now, but not really—Pammy was on the phone with a friend, telling her about this guy who had broken into the apartment the night before. And her friend asked if there was any *good* news. And Pammy said, 'Well, we have food in the house.' Somehow, though, she's been able to deal with all the changes better than Robbie could.

"And my situation has gotten a lot better. I've learned how to handle things. I've learned things that I should have known years ago. I mean I was really unprepared for anything beyond looking for the White Knight. I'm learning all the time. And I feel very proud of how far I've come.

"I feel confident now that whatever happens, I can handle it, I can survive and support my daughter. That's very important. I'm teaching that to Pammy. Even if I suddenly had a lot of money I wouldn't give her a great deal more than she has now. I'm teaching her how to sew her own clothes, to budget what is needed. Like if I want to make curtains I try to buy one rod a week, or one piece of material, sort of spread things out. But eventually they get done.

"We do really simple things together: We go ice skating in the winter, go for walks in the park, teach each other games, read.

"My mother tries to pressure Pam sometimes, in subtle ways. Like she got her this Barbie doll she knew I didn't want her to have. There's such a heavy concentration on the social thing. Barbie goes to the prom. Barbie has a new townhouse. It's setting up the types of values I don't believe in. It just pushes little girls into molds and continues the old myths about women. I saw it happen with my friends. For a while, it happened to me.

"For some women I guess it works. In the subway, I ran into a girl I graduated with. And there we stood, me in jeans, looking younger than I did ten years ago, her in her little pumps and gloves and hat, looking middle-aged. Of course, at first we looked straight at each other and then looked away. Finally I walked over and said, 'How are you, Susan?' She said OK. She and her husband were in town visiting some relatives, and to see a play or something. Her biggest thing was did I know how she could get to Lord and Taylor!

"You know, I used to feel funny about why I'm different than my family and the friends I grew up with. But I've learned to live with it. And I've decided that it keeps me young. I am who I am and I've got to do what feels right for me. I don't apologize anymore to anybody."

JENNY JACKSON

Because we're black, that's one strike against us.

As a child in a time and place when women, to some extent, were still considered property by some men, Jenny Jackson felt the double yoke of growing up female and growing up black.

Jenny was raised mainly by her maternal grandmother because her mother was always working to support Jenny, her two younger sisters, and her younger brother. Jenny's mother, separated from her husband when she was twenty-three, applied for state assistance. Her mother was forced to have her father arrested to try and get some support, which he couldn't pay anyway. So, with an eighth-grade education, no skills, and four children to support, Jenny's mother found the only work available, "in the big people's houses."

"I remember when my mother would go clean up these houses and they'd give her three or four dollars for a whole day's work. And she had to keep saying, 'Yes, ma'am,' and 'No, sir.'"

When her mother went to work, Jenny, only eight but the oldest child, had to take care of her brother and sisters. She saw her mother only a few hours a day and almost never when her mother was rested and in a good mood. Her grandmother, Jenny said, was the only adult she ever felt real affection for. It was her grandmother who taught her how to cook and how to love.

"My first cake, oh my God! It looked like a truck had run over it! It had fallen on both sides, and the frosting was so thin it ran off. But wasn't it delicious, my grandmother said. You couldn't have told it hadn't come from a bakery. According to her, I had baked the President's cake. She made you feel so good about yourself.

"But one day I can remember standing at the door and looking out over the yard and thinking I wanted something different for myself. I didn't know what, but what my mother had just wasn't for me.

"One day my teacher sent me to this restaurant and the restaurant wouldn't let me inside. I was amazed that all these black people were working in the kitchen making up the food, but you couldn't go to the front and get served. I had to go to the window at the back that said COLORED. I began to see the world wasn't how I'd thought it was. It began to get to me.

"When I was a little older, a cop hit me on the back with his blackjack, just 'cause he felt like it. And they had a hearing, but they didn't do anything. He'd been beating up on a whole lot of blacks, and the whites just had the right to do those things then.

"I never liked being second. But I blocked a lot of it out, because in those days there was nothing else to do. I'd see it mostly after visiting relatives in the North. When I'd go back down South it was so evident. As a kid it was hard for me to deal with. It makes me sick to remember. Like I'd travel on the train and talk to white people. Then you'd get to the station and you couldn't all go eat together. They'd go in the places with the nice big tables and you'd have to go somewhere else, standing in these little holes with the garbage stinking. Traveling, I learned a lot."

When she finished high school, Jenny got odd jobs for a year and trained as a beautician, and then saved money to come up North. Jenny married her former husband two years after she arrived in Boston, and they had three children. Over the years, ongoing financial difficulties ate at the marriage, and then Jenny's husband began drinking heavily. The Jacksons have now been separated for three years.

Because she had been working all along, Jenny made a rapid adjustment to life as a single parent. She has problems with money, living in a bad neighborhood, and her children's schools, but she has set clear goals for herself.

"Of course discrimination still goes on here too, but I try to be as positive as I can be—but truthful. I tell my daughters that because we are black, that's one strike against us; because we are female, that's two strikes against us. And because of where we live now, that can also be a strike against us, if we let it. But don't let it. Try not to let it!

"That's why my first goal is to move out of here. It's taking me so long to save. But I'm planning on having my own beauty shop. Right now I'm just working for somebody else, and waiting. But I'm going to have a nice place, in a nice neighborhood, some place good for the kids and me to be. Now what do they learn when they go out to play? The quickest ways to hurt each other. There are too many things the children can pick up here that are grossly against their well-being. They don't even have to be in a bad situation even; all they have to do is look out at it, out the windows, listen to it in the hallways."

Meanwhile Jenny is working on her second goal, which is better schooling for her children. School psychologists have told her that Tommy, her oldest child, has the potential to develop superior intellectual skills, and she wants to put him in a private school.

"In this school, they don't always understand. His teacher asked me once how I discipline Tommy. And I said if we were having dessert he just didn't get any. But to her that was nothing. She said, 'What is that? A deprived dessert, nothing.' But I said, 'For you, most likely coming from a good-income background, to you dessert wouldn't be anything. But to people who don't have the money to buy regular food sometimes, dessert would be everything.'

"And they make judgments. They see you coming and they see you're black, and the teachers, some of them, they IQ you out. Before they found out that Tommy was dyslectic, they put him with retarded children. Some of them were wild or having hallucinations, some were medicated, some couldn't even speak. When he saw the children he refused to go back. They had to drag him in there screaming and yelling every day. He had more sense and intelligence than they in knowing where he didn't belong. He tried to tell me about these strange children, but at first it sounded so crazy I didn't really listen.

"Naturally I couldn't conceive of them putting him in a classroom like that. Finally I did listen and went to the school, so he was taken out of that class and now he's doing really well. But the school's still not good enough. To go to a better one, he has to get a scholarship, and there aren't many.

"One school said they have only three slots open to low-income parents. The thought came to me that maybe the people who were putting the slots in didn't think people whose children were coming from low-income homes have the same rights to a good start as people coming from wealthy sources.

"That to me seems very foolish, because in the future they would have to support these children who don't get a good start. Because children *are* the future. And if you don't provide a good start, then they're not going to have a chance to make it in the world.

"So I have to plan ahead for my daughters too, because being girls they'll have two strikes against them. I don't ever want my kids to think they're less than anyone else; unless they bring that on themselves.

"I never had to discuss prejudice with my kids until the busing issue came up in Boston. I remember Susana must have been about five years old, and she said, 'Why is it they don't want to go to school with us? They don't think they're as good as we are?' I really felt proud. It could easily have been, 'Don't they think we're as good as them?'

"I can't do anything about the racial problems in Boston; but I can teach my kids that there's another way to go in life. I can teach them that, and how to keep loving themselves. I can set higher goals than the ones they see around them. They are going to make it. I'm going to—one way or the other—make sure they do."

KATHY MACDONALD

> I thought all this was happening to me because I wasn't a good person; because good people make it in this country.

Kathy MacDonald is the third of five children who grew up in a predominantly Irish, "lace-curtain" neighborhood. Kathy and her brothers grew up with one foot in the old country and one foot not too firmly planted in the new morals of the sixties. Kathy's mother, a devoutly religious woman, helped shape many of Kathy's early ideas of what she should be in life.

Kathy has many good memories of growing up in her neighborhood and in her parents' home. But many of the values she learned were anchors that held her back for a time, making personal development as a woman difficult, and survival as a single mother difficult also.

Kathy's parents "were extremely proud people—they would

never, never take anything that they didn't work for." At nineteen, Kathy married a man who shared her parents' values— values that led to the disruption of their marriage.

The MacDonalds had two children early in their marriage: a girl, and a boy who was born with a cleft palate and a club foot. These birth defects required extensive and expensive medical attention. But the family had no medical coverage. And rather than apply for Medicaid, Kathy's husband took on a second, part-time job on weekends. Eventually, he took a third job working evenings in a gas station to make ends meet. The strain, however, proved too much for Mr. MacDonald and he had a nervous breakdown.

"Maybe if he had applied for Medicaid he wouldn't have had a breakdown—but see, he could not. It was totally against his system. You are taught to think that 'good people' don't do that.

"Living with him just became unbearable. When he started yelling and screaming a lot, that made it easier to leave him. After four years of marriage I think I knew somehow that it wasn't going to work, but it was hard because of my religion to make the decision to separate. And I had the kids then (aged two and three at the time) and I had no idea what else I'd do, how we'd live.

"He was getting more and more tense 'cause he knew I was going to go and then one night I couldn't stand it anymore and took the kids and went to my friend Eva's.

"Michael wouldn't leave the apartment. He didn't want to separate. He kept calling and saying just come back. But he was violent then and didn't realize that he probably didn't want to be with me either.

"I was scared and it affected my appetite most. I was depressed, afraid nothing would ever be the same. But I knew I couldn't live with him again. It was really a bad time on the kids too. They couldn't understand what was going on, and I wasn't in any shape to explain to them.

"Michael started throwing things at me when he'd see me, and I was really afraid. He finally left the apartment because I threatened that I'd call the police if he didn't get out. So then I went back once he was gone. My parents had no extra money, so there didn't seem to be anything else to do but apply for welfare."

Kathy's parents were appalled, especially her mother, about the breakup of the marriage and the idea of welfare. They made Kathy feel even more guilty than she was already feeling.

"I was raised in that era, when there were these things that my people just didn't do. None of my relatives had ever gotten divorced, and none had ever gone on welfare. So when I had to do that it was like I wasn't a good person. I had really bought that. I can't believe it now, how I felt then. I was afraid my postman, really, was telling all my neighbors that I was getting welfare checks. It made me paranoid.

"I didn't want people to know. People who take a handout have no pride—that's what I believed. I was depressed for a year. That whole time is like a blur—whole months I just can't remember at all. I'd lie on my bed after the kids were asleep and just stare at the ceiling and think, 'How can I do this for fifteen, twenty years? I was just a wreck. I never went anywhere, would just sit alone and brood.

"You know what got me out of it? I got angry. I got good and goddamn angry about how I was punishing myself. For a year I hated myself and everyone else because I had no money. And I was mad I was born a woman. So I got a job waitressing for a while and then I got mad about that too. I couldn't make enough to get off welfare. Why should I have to work for two-fifty an hour, and there's no one to help you, or take care of the kids? It was bad enough to have no father. Why did my kids have no mother too?

"Then all of a sudden it became really clear that you can't go on alone forever. Somebody has to recognize you. You have to get some feedback from somebody, somewhere along the line in a world that's telling you that you are shit all the time; you have to have someone say that you are really neat."

Kathy forced herself to go out to meet other adults and get a break from her kids and her isolation. Soon she met Jack, who began to encourage her. "He saw things in me I just couldn't see at the time." He suggested she go back to school to prepare for a career, and he tried to help her out with the kids and the house. At first, taking courses at a community college—where she applied for tuition aid as a low-income mother—was exhilarating. "The teachers began telling me I was bright and little by little I started to get good feelings about myself back again, to feel like I was a good person, that I wasn't really bad."

But soon Kathy realized that even with Jack's help she was overloaded. "Sometimes I actually beat my head on the floor, feeling I had to be beat and punished. I was still so guilty about being on welfare, and now about the tuition aid too. One day I had to tell my teacher, 'Sometimes when you're lecturing, I'm really not there; I'm flying around the room and stuff.'" The teacher thought Kathy should see a psychologist and made an appointment for her.

"He said I was spending so much energy that I was physically weak. It was really the internal anger, the anger of thinking I was screwed, that got me where I am. I had to get the anger out, to fight. I had to fight to get places where some other people got to naturally. All the time trying to prove I was just as good as other people."

Kathy is now about to share an apartment with her boyfriend. In addition to the increased intimacy both she and Jack want, it would give her a chance to save some money by cutting rent expenses. Her mother objects. "My mother tells me I'll be living in sin, that she will never come to see me if I move in with Jack. He's also Protestant, and that kills her."

But Kathy is over feeling guilty because she can't live like her mother. She's going to move in with Jack anyway and hope her mother will eventually get over it, because she feels it's the best course for her own life right now.

"I didn't plan on being a single mother. When I got married I thought it was going to be this picket fence and rose garden thing, forever, you know? But I learned that nothing is forever, and you've got to work with what you've got, to be able to change when things don't go the way you've planned. I've learned that some things just aren't my fault, but you've got to live with them the best you can. Besides me, I've got to think about the kids. They like Jack and need a father.

"I'm sorry my mother feels the way she does. It doesn't make it easy for either of us. But she's living in the past and I'm trying to live today."

EXPANDING POSSIBILITIES

Many women we talked to at the Stress and Families Project felt they could really understand their mothers, why they had lived, or were now living, their lives in the ways they did. But not one woman mentioned a desire to repeat her mother's life. Despite the things women perceive as harder today, the 1980s offers women more than ever before. Among the most-often cited blessings of the 1980s—those changes that have expanded women's life possibilities—are:

Personal freedom. "I have more options; my mother could only have done one thing—stay home."

Time-saving mechanical conveniences. "My mother had a wood stove. Now there are laundromats, but my mother used to scrub by hand or use this old ringer washer."

Personal identity. "My mother could never develop herself or her own interests; she had no support or encouragement to do that."

New expectations for intimate relations. "My mother lived with a lot of really unacceptable behavior from her husband. Things younger women today just wouldn't put up with."

Employment opportunities. "You can find jobs now that just weren't available for women a generation ago. And there are now government agencies to see that employers don't discriminate anymore."

Increasing use of day-care centers. "Raising kids alone was a lot harder than it is now. Nowadays a lot of mothers use pre-schools, but then there was no day care, and we were taught it was wrong to have outsiders take care of your kids."

Increasing social networks and communication with other women. "I get a lot of support my mother didn't get, from organizations like Parents Anonymous, Respond, Infants at Risk, from babysitters and friends. I make use of them every day."

Old values die hard; and some women's mothers—caught in their own eras and stereotypes—are not the resources of wisdom and comfort they could be in directing their daughters' progress in a new society.

From whatever background, women are dealing daily—sometimes alone—with society's efforts to program their behavior and their images of themselves. Often discrimination—racial, ethnic, religious, or sexist—plays a part in anchoring women in the past.

No matter what the source of these anchors, each single mother has to work out her own redefinition of herself. All single mothers are asking the same questions: "How do I deal with my past? How do I plan for the future? And where do I find the strength to get where I want to go?"

Sometimes it is necessary to cut the most binding ties in order to sail free. This is more easily accomplished when women talk out common problems with each other. In doing so, it is often easier for women to see themselves as a great resource, as pioneers raising the world's future generation.

CHAPTER SEVEN

Time Management: Making Every Minute Count

How much time do you get for yourself each day, to spend as you would like?

—*Stress and Families interviewer*

About one hour a day, if I get up at five-thirty.

—POLLY SIMON

One hour a day isn't a lot of free time for a mother working two jobs. But Polly Simon tries to make every minute of it count. Divorced for three years, Polly is a twenty-nine-year-old single mother who supports her three children as a legal secretary. Her paid job (forty hours a week and sometimes weekend work) is taxing. Between it and her thirty-hour-a-week unpaid job as mother of two boys (aged six and a half and eight) and a five-year-old daughter, she is often left wishing for an extra eight hours in each day.

"I'm constantly on the go," Polly said. "Really, I'm twice as busy as I was when I was married and John was supporting us. I like my job but it is very demanding. And my boss has a fit if I'm two minutes late. So I have to make sure I get out on time every morning.

"I wish I could just throw on a pair of jeans some mornings; it would be much simpler. But the firm is very strict about a dress code so I have to take the time to look the part—makeup perfect and the whole thing. I'm also very conscious of food. I hate processed stuff and usually make the boys' lunches to make sure they're not eating junk foods. It all takes time. It used to be that I was in a mad dash all day from the time I woke up until I fell into bed at night.

"During the past year, I've discovered the joy of having an hour each morning before the 'first round' begins. I really depend on that. I get up around five-thirty when the kids are still sleeping. And I do a few minutes of light breathing. I learned that in a yoga course. It clears my thoughts and gets rid of this tension I wake up with sometimes. I just breathe out really slow, then breathe in while I clear my head. I do it for about ten minutes before I have a bath and something light for breakfast—usually an egg, some fruit, and toast. While I'm sitting there I just listen to the quiet and make plans for the day.

"At first I sometimes overslept. When I started late and didn't have that hour to myself I'd be cranky all day. Once I realized how badly I needed that time for myself, it's been no sacrifice at all to get up early."

What made the difference in Polly's day was using time-management skills. Using charts to analyze her activities and her reactions to them, she was able to reprogram her time and to improve the overall quality of her days.

Many single mothers are now, like Polly, working at full-time jobs outside the home. Some have found part-time work, and others are still deciding what work paths to pursue. Regardless of how you now spend a typical day, you will find life more enjoyable if you have:

- Some time off, routinely, from the demands of raising children and
- Some control over how your time is spent each day.

These two things are very important for your well-being. Those women interviewed who were unable to exercise control over their time, and to relax from child-care responsibilities periodically, were more likely to show symptoms of poor mental health.

TIME OFF

Whether it's eating ice cream, running a company, or raising children, too much of anything can be a bad thing. Any one activity turns monotonous and stressful without a little variety. That's why everyone needs to "get away from it all" every now and then, even women who prefer full-time child care to work outside the home. This can be hard for some women to admit, especially when our society still expects women to accept full or major responsibility for raising children.

Loveable as children are, they are also demanding, in many ways more demanding than adults. Their needs can be insatiable unless some guidelines are set and the quality of time spent with them is kept positive. Mothers often find that taking short sabbaticals from parenting is the best way of renewing their energy.

Because of the two-job nature of single parenting, nearly half of the women interviewed said they feel they spend too much time with their children, or that the time they spend with them is not always well spent. Finding your limit, and knowing when to take a break from the routine, is essential.

Women who have nearby extended families may find it easiest to relieve themselves of child-care pressures from time to time, but other women rely on babysitters or a babysitting pool to get away for at least an hour or an afternoon, on a regular basis. (For more information on get-away possibilities see Chapter 8.)

PERSONAL CONTROL

To have control over time, so that you can spend some part of your day precisely as you wish, is a second essential for a single mother. One key to time satisfaction is to fit individual, personal needs into each day, whether this is an hour out for a romantic novel or a walk in the woods. Women with the busiest schedules need this personal time the most. The nine-point health plan outlined in Chapter 4 offers some guidelines. But just how are you going to fit some get-it-together time, that important midday body-toning break, and all of the other necessary activities into your day?

Planning Tools

Using some of the simplified techniques of a professional efficiency expert can help. Efficiency experts note the time it takes to get certain tasks done, then decide how those tasks might be rearranged, restructured, or even eliminated. This is exactly what you can do with the help of a Daily Activities Chart.

When a group of executives meet in the home office of a large company to hear reports on the company's progress, graphs and charts are usually drawn up to show just how the company is doing, where it is healthy, and where it needs some adjusting. Without these graphic tools it would be a lot more difficult to plan the next month's activities. In fact, without an overview, the company structures might appear chaotic. Being able to map on charts what is happening makes things clearer.

In the same way, your own life can seem chaotic without an overview of it. That is why making some notes about your own situation will be very helpful and why an Activities Chart is included in this chapter. Once you can see more clearly where you and all family members are, it will be much easier to see where you want to go and how to get there.

Completing Your Chart:

On the following page is a time chart very much like the ones completed for each woman interviewed by the Stress and Families Project. Plan to fill it in before you finish reading this chapter or whenever you have the most uninterrupted time in your day. It is designed to let you look at where you are right now. It will also pinpoint the places in your day where time can be restructured to give you more control and personal satisfaction tomorrow.

1. Turn to the chart on page 108. It is divided into twenty-four hours, beginning at 4 A.M. Each hour is notched with lines that indicate quarter hours. To the right of each hour there is space for you to write in:

• The activities you are normally involved in each hour of the day;
• The names of others—children, friends, or relatives—who may be involved with you in each activity;
• A rating of how much you enjoy or dislike each activity.

2. Beginning with the time you usually rise each morning during the week, write in "Wake up" in the appropriate slot. Then follow through on a typical day, filling in each activity— whatever it is you are physically doing during that time. It may be washing, preparing breakfast, waking the children, performing work inside or outside your home, watching television, visiting with neighbors, and so on. Be as exact as you can.

Obviously you don't do exactly the same things every day of your life, but try to pick a "typical day" during the week. If your days are very different—for example if you work three days a week and stay home two days a week—you may want to make a copy of the Activities Chart so you can analyze both types of days. Fill in the day as thoroughly as you can. When it isn't possible to be exact, estimate an average time for a particular task. For instance, if evening shopping takes you anywhere from twenty minutes to forty minutes, write in thirty minutes.

3. Beside each activity, fill in the names of the people who are with you as you complete the activity. For example, if you make breakfast when all your children are present, then include their names beside "Breakfast." If you are by yourself, write "Self."

4. Last, give each event a one to six Enjoyment Rating. One means *most* enjoyable activities of the day; three is neutral; six means you hate it. Be as accurate as you can. Sometimes it is easiest to rate the most favorite and least favorite first. Then you may be more clear about those tasks you are not emotionally involved in; give those a three rating.

DAILY ACTIVITIES CHART (1)

Time	Activities	Those Involved (Self—Others)	Enjoyment Rating (1–6)	Time	Activities	Those involved (Self—Others)	Enjoyment Rating (1–6)
4 A.M.				4 P.M.			
5 A.M.				5 P.M.			
6 A.M.				6 P.M.			
7 A.M.				7 P.M.			
8 A.M.				8 P.M.			
9 A.M.				9 P.M.			
10 A.M.				10 P.M.			
11 A.M.				11 P.M.			
NOON				MIDNIGHT			
1 P.M.				1 A.M.			
2 P.M.				2 A.M.			
3 P.M.				3 A.M.			

Once you have completed your chart, take a few minutes to do a quick Organizational Assessment.

ASSESSMENT

A) Add up Personnel Distribution (whom you are doing what with)

Total Time Spent with Children	*No. of Hours*	*Are you Satisfied/Not Satisfied with This Time Distribution?* (Check One)	
		Sat.	*Not Sat.*
Child A	_____		
Child B	_____	_____	_____
Child C	_____		
_____	_____		
_____	_____		
_____	_____		
_____	_____		
_____	_____		
Total No. of Hours with Children	_____		

Total Time Spent with Other Adults	*No. of Hours*	*Sat.*	*Not Sat.*
Adult A	_____	_____	_____
Adult B	_____		
Adult C	_____		
_____	_____		
_____	_____		
_____	_____		
_____	_____		
Total No. of Hours with Adults	_____		

Total Time Spent Alone	_____	*Sat.*	*Not Sat.*
		_____	_____

Total Hours
Spent

B) *Most Pleasant Activities* _____

_____

_____

_____

_____

_____

_____

_____

C) *Least Pleasant Activities* _____

_____

_____

_____

_____

_____

D) *Most Stressful Parts of
   the Day*   E) *Most Free Time*
   From ____ to ____   From ____ to ____
   From ____ to ____   From ____ to ____

Finding Your Patterns

Once you have filled in your chart you will be able to see one of your typical days a little more clearly. Take a good look at it. What patterns do you see? Which activities are taking up most of your time? And how do you feel about them? Which are most enjoyable? Which are the least enjoyable? Does this divide your days into highs and lows? And what about "other" contacts? How much time do you spend with other people (adults and children) and how much time do you have left just for yourself?

Once you discover the patterns in your chart you will begin to see:

- Spots in your day where you can take a litttle more control over how your time is spent;

- How you will be able to use that control to (1.) tone down some of the high-stress, frantic rush times and (2.) plan in some more personal time for health and pleasure activities.

Reprogramming

Ask yourself what you want to 'reprogram' the most as you look at your chart and review a typical day. Notice what kinds of gut feelings you get as you think about each portion of your day. Note the areas of most tension. Full-time working mothers may find that the time of most "activities overlap" is when the nine to five work day runs into the beginning of the "second job" (usually between 4 P.M. and 6 or 7 P.M.). Early mornings can also be a time of chaos—when everyone is running behind schedule and needs ten things done at once while you try to get breakfast ready. At times like these, things can get very tense.

Energy Cycles How you begin to reprogram your most hectic times depends on your own personal energy cycles. Before rearranging your schedule you should note when your physical and emotional peaks occur most naturally during the day. Some women, like Pam Johnson, are "in a fog until nine or ten A.M." Pam says, "I just can't seem to get myself together early in the morning—I can hardly find the coffeepot." Other women, like Polly Simon, are natural early risers; they are up with the birds and feel energetic as soon as they wake.

You are probably already aware of your daily peaks and valleys, but a look at your completed chart should eliminate any doubts. Note the least-liked events in your day, the ones that cause you the most stress or other unpleasant feelings. Now try to sort out whether you really dislike these tasks or just have to cope with them when you have too little energy. Often there is some combination of both.

Polly, for instance, hated 5 P.M. A look at her chart indicated that she had a dozen separate tasks to complete at that hour while she was shifting gears from her outside job to her second job of parenting and housekeeping. That in itself was a strain. What made it worse was that Polly was trying to get these dozen things done when she was feeling at her lowest point in the day. The activities overlap was making most weekday dinner hours a family disaster.

Here is what would happen. Often stressed until the final minute by a zealous, demanding boss, Polly would rush out of her office building to face the commuter jam at her subway stop. She would board an overcrowded subway sardined together with other commuters. Arriving home, Polly would open the door of her apartment to greet her children. Each would immediately clamor for her attention, wanting to relate all the day's happenings above a blaring television, while her babysitter inevitably began a long-winded monologue. Polly's teenage sitter would, more often than not, hang around to continue her monologue while Polly swept up the floor and the rest of the afternoon's disorder (sometimes contributed by her sitter as well as the children), did a quick washup of the day's accumulated dishes, set a hurried table, and began dinner. All the while in full motion, Polly would try to comment on her sitter's latest romantic problems while answering questions from her children. Details often seemed overwhelming and endless before Polly could collapse into a chair. Then she would cithor wolf down her food or sit and look at it, wondering where her appetite had gone, and how much a ticket to the Caribbean would cost.

Polly had known for some time that she hated the weekday hours from five to six. But not until she tried to jam all her activities into the space on her chart did she realize how justified her feelings were. Unknowingly, she had been trying to be superwoman; and it wasn't working. With the facts in front of her, she could begin to take more control of her time.

Controlling the Logjams   Whatever time of day your own personal activity overlaps occur, you can begin to make more efficient (and less stressful) use of time by taking into account your natural highs and lows, and analyzing the activities that are causing the jam-ups. To do this:

1. Make a very detailed list of each task that you are currently doing during a high-stress time. (Check your Daily Activities Chart and, if necessary, use extra paper to be even more specific in listing everything you are trying to do at that time.)

2. Next, underline how many of these tasks *have* to be accomplished at this time. For instance, the children have to have clothes to wear to school each day. But are you looking for them each morning *just* before the bus leaves? Can you make sure on Sunday afternoon that clothes are ready for the week—or at least do this the evening before? Do the breakfast dishes have to be washed before you leave for work, or would it be easier to leave them soaking and do them with the dinner dishes—or even to use paper plates and cups?

3. Circle those items that can be done at another time—a time in your day when you have either more energy or less to do. And right now, add those tasks at a new time on the New Activities Chart provided on the following page.

4. And it's very important to decide what someone besides you can take care of. Many mothers do a number of things that their children could easily do for themselves. While children develop at slightly different rates, mothers have often become so used to taking control that they fail to allow their children responsibility for simple tasks that would eliminate some of their own excess jobs: putting toys away, clearing the table, leaving dirty dishes to be rinsed in the sink. Use a manager's approach and discuss with your children at a family council how jobs should be delegated to other family members.

Negotiating with children may not be easy if you have not been teaching them to take much responsibility on a routine basis, but even toddlers will willingly do small chores like throwing things in the garbage if they are praised and made to feel useful. Putting a little thought and effort into explaining the need for help and expressing appreciation will go a long

NEW ACTIVITIES CHART

Time	Activities	Those Involved (Self—Others)	Enjoyment Rating (1-6)	Time	Activities	Those involved (Self—Others)	Enjoyment Rating (1-6)
4 A.M.				4 P.M.			
5 A.M.				5 P.M.			
6 A.M.				6 P.M.			
7 A.M.				7 P.M.			
8 A.M.				8 P.M.			
9 A.M.				9 P.M.			
10 A.M.				10 P.M.			
11 A.M.				11 P.M.			
NOON				MIDNIGHT			
1 P.M.				1 A.M.			
2 P.M.				2 A.M.			
3 P.M.				3 A.M.			

way in enlisting your children's cooperation. Pointing out the mutual benefits to be gained is important. Assigning tasks often gives toddlers a sense of grown-upness. For instance, Polly might say, "I'd appreciate a little help now so we can get these things out of the way and have some time to talk." Or, "I can't listen as easily when I'm flying around doing ten things. If you help out with the table now, then we can relax together." Older children often resent orders and assignments and respond more cooperatively if you allow them to participate in choosing their own chores. Show them your Daily Activities Chart and let them rate how much *they* enjoy or dislike each activity. Perhaps they will volunteer to do chores you hate. If not, the discussion will allow you to communicate—without seeming to complain—what you are up against. Such communication can encourage a sense of fairness and generosity in children, making them willing to share even the unpleasant tasks. Once your children are clear about your own goals, and sure that this is a pattern you are setting for a sensible purpose, things should run much more smoothly. You may have some failures in the beginning, but ignore them and stick to what you started. Eventually it will work. Make sure your children do not assume tasks that are too onerous for them or they will be discouraged and feel they are a hindrance rather than a help. If you have very young children, they will be able to do only very simple things like washing a cucumber, and you will have to wait a bit before they can be a true help. But it is still good for them to have the feeling they are sharing the family work. And if you have more than one child, spread the work around as evenly as possible. That will leave you more time for the major things your children cannot help out with.

In addition to the ways your children might be helping out, what about other adults in your family? What about your child-care helper or local babysitter? Would it be worth another ten dollars or so a week to request some slight help that might make your crunch times easier?

And if you are currently sharing space with a male friend, do remember that the relationship should be mutually beneficial; he should be carrying his own part of the household responsibilities. Many men don't share work simply because women don't expect them to.

5. Accept that some unpleasant events and some stresses are unavoidable. (No one likes taking out the garbage, and you do have to balance the checkbook now and then.) But try to rearrange some of the unpleasant tasks to fit in with your high-energy times instead of further weighting down your low-energy ebbs. The pile of dishes in the sink, for instance, may look twice as high at 6 P.M. as at 8 when you've had a chance to unwind a bit.

6. Last, cross out tasks that really don't need to be done at all. There may be few of these, but often there is something that just doesn't have to be done (or done with the frequency you are now putting into it). Many women would prefer to clean their kitchen corners with a toothbrush, make a daily or weekly cleaning tour of the tops of cabinets and refrigerator, or insist on ironing towels. Ask yourself what you may be just a little compulsive about. If it makes you happy to scrub the sink each morning, then fine. But if it takes five minutes away from the time when you could be sitting with your feet up catching a breath after the children leave for school, then maybe you could try living with a few more germs and a little less stress.

Once you have made a thorough assessment—transferring those circled "do it another time" items, reassigning some tasks to other people when possible, rescheduling the really unpleasant tasks, and crossing off any that you can—you should begin to feel a little less chaotic tomorrow morning, or tomorrow evening. Once you see how much more smoothly you can run your day, you will never slide back into unplanned chaos.

It will take a little thought and effort to break some habits and get into new ones. Start with one thing at a time. Here's how Polly applied some of these techniques to her end-of-day-disaster hour.

The Way It Could Be

By arranging with her sitter to extend child-care activities for an extra five to ten minutes each day, Polly made a whole new beginning to her evenings. Rather than rushing from outside chaos to inside chaos, Polly would open her door and say, "Hi, it's good to be home; I love you but give me a few minutes to catch my breath." By giving her children a snack to tide them over until dinner (something nourishing and nonfilling, like a glass of milk and a piece of fruit), Polly found she could forestall the Impatient Hungers and make cooperation a little more likely.

Getting out of her work clothes, she would head for the bathroom and a quick pick-me-up shower and a change into something more comfortable. Even a few minutes alone did wonders for that in-between-jobs transition time. And getting out of her work clothes helped put that part of the day behind her a little faster.

Such a transition time is easier to arrange if you have an in-home sitter, but if not, a new routine could be set up by having an older child watch the younger ones, or by asking a friend or neighbor in your building for a few minutes of sitter time (perhaps in exchange for doing her some favor that would not inconvenience you).

Refreshed, and intent on making the dinner hour a pleasant experience, Polly would leave the day's dishes until after dinner and begin preparing food (often one-dish meals prepared on weekends and frozen for later) while her older son, aged eight, helped clear off the table and set some paper plates and silverware.

Polly's other children did the tasks they had chosen at a family council, leaving Polly free to begin dinner without excess chatter and confusion. Often she had time for predinner hugs before sitting down to enjoy her food and her children with half the stress of her previous, unmanaged evenings.

Polly's talkative sitter responded favorably when Polly diplomatically suggested a restructuring of their time together. To avoid the sitter's chatter, which was distracting when she was trying to make dinner, Polly said, "That sounds really interesting and I'd like to talk to you about it but I just can't focus on what you are saying right now with everything else I have to do. I'd love to get together Tuesday evening when the kids are in bed and we can both relax. Why don't you come over about eight-thirty?"

Restructuring time with "hanger-on friends" can often be managed more smoothly than we think unless the person is totally unreasonable—in which case you might want to reevaluate the relationship all together. In Polly's case, she needed and was pleased with her friend overall. Eliminating the friendship would not have been advisable. With firmness, kindness, clear goals, and good timing she was able to renegotiate the friendship so it did not conflict with her most pressing needs.

PLANNING NEW GOALS

1. To improve your health basics, first decide where tomorrow's Quiet Morning Time is going to come from. Rethink your typical morning with the eye of an efficiency expert (one who is streamlining the duties of a VIP). Turn to your new Daily Activities Chart and write in at least ten minutes of QMT.

You may have to:

- Set your alarm a little earlier;
- Eliminate part of the morning's hassles by completing some tasks the evening before, or on weekends;
- Assign a few chores to someone else;
- Let some things go for now.

Don't worry if all does not go according to plan at first. The baby may decide to get up early also, the phone may ring and you may have to take a call you can't cut short. But once you make the initial attempt, sooner or later a regulated day will become a pattern. When that happens you will probably wonder how you ever managed to start your day differently.

2. Once you have established a more relaxed morning pattern (this should take anywhere from a few days to a week or so), systematically reevaluate the rest of your day. Taking one step at a time, begin to reshuffle the activities in your day. Try to make room for a midday body toning and the rest of your physical and emotional needs, on a routine basis.

3. Refer back to Chapter 4 at least once a week for your basic body needs. You will need some reminders of your goals, just to begin breaking old habits. By the end of your third and fourth week you should very definitely be feeling the positive effects of your time management. You should be routinely including in your day: QMT, a midday body break, a smoother, less stressed dinner hour, more enjoyable family time, and a relaxed evening hour just before bedtime.

As you accomplish your goals, write them in on your new chart. And give yourself a big pat on the back. Even if you succeed in gaining only an extra five or ten minutes here and there in those time slots, it is valuable time you didn't have before. Even small doses of less stressed time and more controlled activities will have huge payoffs in how you're going to feel. Your body will be stronger, your mind clearer; and the whole world is going to seem a little nicer place to be living in.

TIPS TO REMEMBER

- Set priorities for task division at a family council as soon as possible. (See Chapter 8 for approaches to democratic home discussions.)
- Keep your eyes open for time-saving new products, such as iron-on tape and patches that eliminate the need for hemming and sewing clothes.
- Use your high-energy times for tasks you often put off because they are unpleasant.

- Pamper yourself during low-energy times—so that you can avoid overload and losing your temper.

- Don't feel guilty about saying you need some time to yourself— everyone needs it; why shouldn't you?

- Whenever possible, combine errands outside the home to conserve time and gas.

- Keep a list of items that are running low. This will eliminate the last-minute rush to the corner store for the spaghetti sauce you thought was on the back shelf. Keep a list on the refrigerator or bulletin board and have your children use it too (or tell you when they've eaten the last of the breakfast cereal if they are too young to write).

- Eliminate unnecessary or tiresome invasions of your privacy. Learn to say "No, thank you, I don't need any" to telephone solicitors, or "I'll call you back when I have some time" to too chatty friends. You might even try leaving the phone off the hook during your busiest times.

- Make it a point to check out your library for books full of time- and money-saving ideas for busy mothers. Get the big thick copy of *Hints from Heloise,* for example, and spend a few evenings noting the most useful suggestions. (This book includes everything from how to recycle leftovers and what to do with your mesh onion bags to how to quickly burglar-proof a broken window lock.) *How to Live Cheap but Good* includes some good, quick meal preparation tips, how-to's on home repairs, and suggestions for fixing up a new apartment without spending your next six months' wages. There are numerous other books available that can help you streamline necessary but detestable chores.

References

Dill, Diana, and Elizabeth Greywolf. "Daily Lives," *Lives in Stress: Women and Depression,* ed. D. Belle. Beverly Hills, Calif: Sage, 1982.

Heloise, *Hints from Heloise,* New York: Arbor House, 1980.

Proiss, Martin. *How to Live Cheap but Good,* New York: American Heritage Press, 1971.

CHAPTER EIGHT

Keys to Creative Parenting

When I became a single parent I really didn't know how to do it—how to be both a mother and father to my kids. I learned by seeing how other people waste their lives. I thought, 'Nope, I'm not going that route. I have willpower, and patience.' And believe me, I use both.

—ANNA BRESLOW

Without patience and willpower, no single mother can succeed at the tough job cut out for her. But when patience is stretched beyond normal limits it's hard to locate the willpower that has worked magic for you in the past. Every now and then you are bound to feel you've lost control, that you are no longer being the loving and understanding mother you would like to be.

When you experience what could be called a "blot-out" of your normal personality, you may feel swallowed by rage or by depression, reacting with dramatic mood and behavior changes. Your reactions may vary from being rude and unpleasant to saying and doing things that can be harmful to you and to your children.

If you experience a mild form of blot-out, the damage may not be too hard to repair; bursting out with a sudden unkind word or smashing a dish is not the end of the world. But if unrelieved stress or depression is intense enough, or becomes chronic, damage is apt to be more serious. You may be unable to give your children the daily doses of affection and attention they need to stay healthy; you may even lash out in physical assault.

Fortunately, most parents—single or not—never reach this level. But every mother has days when the potential for burnout is too close for comfort, when the old coping strategies just don't seem to work anymore. How can you make sure your family life stays safe and sane? How can you consistently be the kind of parent your child needs?

- By learning to recognize danger signs, and
- By practicing parenting skills that help increase your child's self-esteem, and your own.

DANGER SIGNS

"Do you spend less time, as much time, or more time than you would like with your children?"

Almost half of the women interviewed by the Stress and Family Project said they spend more time with their children than they would like. Because children can be extremely demanding, and babysitting fees can seem an extravagance, this response is quite understandable. But sometimes mothers feel guilty about taking time out for themselves when they have been told the measure of a mother is the amount of time she spends at home. Consider these two families.

Betty Martin lets everyone know she is there for her children "when they need me." She is home, in fact, twenty-four hours a day. But Betty feels a lot of financial pressures, is upset with her inability to find employment, and has not resolved her anger with her former husband. Unthinkingly, Betty passes on anger to her kids by nagging them for the smallest misbehavior—letting them know in a hundred ways that the only time she ever gets any peace and quiet is when they are in bed. Recently she has started to have a cocktail or two in the middle of the day and tunes her children out while she tunes the soap operas in.

Anna Breslow works full time at a hectic supervisory job for a local utilities company. She must get up at 6 A.M. every morning and doesn't get home until twelve hours later. She has only about four hours a night for her children before they go to bed. But when Anna gets home she is almost always glad to see her children. The family exchanges stories about what happened at work, school, and play before she reads the children a story and puts them to bed.

It isn't hard to guess which mother is enjoying her job of parenting more, and which children are feeling better about themselves.

Often the misguided assumption that a mother should be there for her children at all times leads to inner resentment. Then, because society tells her she isn't supposed to resent her children, she stuffs the angry feelings down. She may be totally unaware that her feelings are surfacing in a hundred indirect ways.

	TRUE	FALSE
Do you find yourself frequently tense and irritable?	____	____
Do you often feel you are losing control of the situation?	____	____
Do you often pick at your children, dwelling on what they are doing wrong, rather than praising what they do well?	____	____
Do you react to minor situations with dramatic mood swings and punishment, find yourself apologizing after the fact?	____	____
Do you rely consistently on alcohol or drugs to get you through a day?	____	____
Do you spend more time in your home than you want to and resent other people their apparent freedom?	____	____

If the answers to these questions are yes, it is likely it has been some time since you heard your child really laughing. And longer still since you and your child have laughed together.

If this is the case, you should take corrective action immediately. Seek help from friends, relatives, or other women in support groups with whom you can share concerns and learn new ways of coping with your problems.

If you feel your problems have gone beyond those that can be handled by informal help, call a local health center or hotline service, seek referral through your physician, or contact a private therapist. If you have ever assaulted your child, get help immediately—for your child's sake and your own. Childhelp, a California-based organization, has established a toll-free, national hot line, which is available for parents who abuse—or fear they will soon abuse—their children. It is 1-800-4-A-CHILD.

Everyone can break through destructive patterns of behavior. But it doesn't happen without taking a first step in the right direction.

THE SECRET NO ONE TALKED ABOUT

> We women have been left to think that if we have mixed feelings about accepting the consuming bond to our children we are less than adequate women and mothers. For our well-being and adjustment we need to admit the many emotions we feel in becoming a parent.
> —*THE BOSTON WOMEN'S HEALTH BOOK COLLECTIVE*

Many women have been unable to deal directly with problems that arise from having children because they believe there should be no problems in the first place. Motherhood has been advertised as the most natural job in the world: Most women do it, right? So it can't be all that tough, right? This is the attitude a lot of men take to having children. And when parenting is handled in isolation, there is little opportunity to compare notes. In fact, there has been something of a taboo about even admitting you may not feel totally comfortable handling all facets of motherhood.

After months of pregnancy and the trauma of labor, a woman becomes a mother. Just as she is experiencing physical exhaustion and emotional upheaval, she is presented with an infant who poses many new and frightening responsibilities. How should s/he be held and fed, and how often? What does it mean when your infant cries for no apparent reasons? What do you do about sudden rashes, a fit of choking, vomiting, or diarrhea? Why do infants have dramatic shifts in sleeping and waking patterns? Even with a loving and supportive husband, the first few months can spell upheaval. A baby challenges hidden resources and drastically alters your life. With a second child, fears lessen but the workload is considerably increased.

Although problems and conflicting emotions arise naturally in coping with parenthood, many women have been made to feel as if the strains are due to their inadequacies as women. A "real woman" should be able to handle motherhood effortlessly. Such myths can have a devastating effect on self-esteem.

In *The Future of Motherhood,* sociologist Jessie Bernard discusses some of the reasons why motherhood can be such a difficult undertaking.

- Most women do not freely choose to become mothers. Often children are born as "accidents"—on the automatic assumption one will have children as a natural extension of marriage—before women have a fully developed sense of who they are.

- The majority of men and women have inadequate preparation for parenting responsibilities. Babies do not come with training manuals, and few women have taken courses on child development or are even prepared for the basics of care and feeding.

- Even if women have received some training, few are aware of the major changes children make in an adult's life. Until recently there have been few support networks to ease the transition to parenthood.

- Child care, as vital as it is, has been denigrated by society. Recent studies show that even today, most husbands do not take an active responsibility for sharing the gut work of parenting. They may occasionally play with their children, but do not, typically, share in changing diapers or feeding and cleaning children, participate in toilet training, or walk the floor in the middle of the night.

Because child care is subtly, or not so subtly, perceived as low-level labor (even professional child-care workers are usually badly underpaid), mothers are not viewed as valued, contributing members of society. They come to undervalue their role ("I'm only a mother, only a housewife"). It has been difficult for women to feel consequential as mothers when only "male qualities" (aggression, competition, and intellectual achievement at the expense of emotional development) have been recognized as important ones.

Recently women have begun to question the effects on society of undervaluing the qualities of openness, affection, sharing, and nurturing. But before changes can occur widely within groups, changes must occur within individuals. The family is the basic place to begin.

DEFINING YOUR GOALS

What do you use as a yardstick to measure your success as a parent? Are you doing a good job if you can provide enough food? If your child doesn't talk back to you or fight with other children or get into trouble with the law? Looks physically healthy? If you are providing educational opportunities and your child gets A's on her report card? If you can afford to buy new toys and fashionable clothes?

Food, warm, safe shelter, clean clothes, toys, and a good education are essential for children. But most mothers recognize other, less tangible, needs as equally important. "I want my daughter to feel better about herself than I did growing up." "I want my son to like himself and to treat women with respect." "I don't want my son to be afraid, to know that he can make it, not to let being black hold him back." A mother wants her child to go through life with confidence, without continuing fears that he or she will not make it, will not be liked by others, or will fail at whatever she or he decides to do. Confident individuals are rarer than we would like, proving that instilling confidence is no easy task. As a parent you don't want your children to be braggarts, constantly talking about how successful they are. Nor do you want your children to exhibit other signs of insecurity such as putting others down to make themselves look good, or trying to outcompete. Children on their way to confident adulthood go quietly about their lives, seemingly sure that they are on the right path. They are happy with themselves and proud of their accomplishments. This makes them open and helpful toward others when aid is asked of them. Older children sometimes volunteer help because they understand themselves and others so well, and because they realize that sometimes it is hard to ask for assistance. Their generosity springs from within, because they are people who love themselves. How can you start your children on the road to self-confidence? How can you increase the odds that your child will become a fully functioning, contributing individual?

KEYS TO SUCCESSFUL PARENTING

The keys to confident and creative parenting can be found in:
Self-help—strengthening your inner coping resources.
Community support—creating an effective network of support for temporary or ongoing parenting concerns.
Education—becoming an informed parent, one who knows, for example, the developmental stages her child will go through, so that expectations for behavior are realistic and compatible with her child's abilities.
Confidence in yourself as a parent releases your ability to vitalize your child and enhance his self-image. When your child is feeling good about himself he is able to respond to you in more open and loving ways. Positive feelings then snowball;

your family is working together instead of living in isolated units.

Building in Balance

Each generation of parents tries, for the most part, to raise its children in the best ways possible. But what is considered "best" varies enormously. Our grandparents took the firm approach, often translated as Parents Know Best just because they are parents. The permissive approach of the sixties, probably an attempt to correct the imbalances of the previous generation, was equally one-sided, often ending as Children Know Best. Permissiveness is blamed today for the "me generation," concerned only with themselves, who feel society owes them all they ask, whether or not they pay any dues.

Both of these approaches were extreme because they failed to consider the needs of children and parents together. When parenting is viewed as one side holding all the cards, or none of them, the family is divided into camps. For the single mother, this can mean your living room feels like a battleground in which dramas are enacted between Me and Them, with uneasy truces in between.

Your own and your children's human rights can be met through negotiation and compromise. By establishing one fundamental, workable goal for your family—fostering self-esteem in yourself and in your children—you can lay the groundwork for an increasingly happy, satisfying homelife together.

Does your child respect herself and feel loved? Dorothy Corkville Briggs, in *Your Child's Self-Esteem,* suggests that the single most essential ingredient in your child's development is high self-esteem (the feeling one is valued because s/he is a human being, that s/he has inherent worth and is loved). This book is highly recommended for its step-by-step approach to getting into a child's shoes and helping her or him establish a healthy self-image. Many of the particular problems you encounter as a parent, Briggs feels, are simply symptoms of the lack of self-esteem in your child—or sometimes in yourself.

Ways to ensure your child gets a daily dose of this essential emotional nutrient will be discussed throughout this chapter. But to help your child feel loved and worthwhile, you've got to begin with a double-check on your own self-esteem. A basic rule of giving is that you can't give what you don't have.

PARENTING KEY NO. 1—SELF-HELP

> One night I just lost it. I was feeling so tired I wanted to die, so upset with Bobby waking and crying every night. My friend Jean called and I couldn't even speak to her. She came over and held me, just held me and hugged me for an hour while I cried. Bobby woke up again in the middle of the night and this time I was able to go to him and hug him and give him back some of the love I'd gotten.

Every mother needs a private place to retreat, a comfortable and pleasant place to rest and renew herself. This doesn't mean only a physical place—a "room of one's own"—but the place inside ourselves where we are most centered and calm.

Sometimes others can lead us back there, as when a friend hugs us, and sometimes, given sufficient time and energy, we can get there on our own. But the longer we are absent from that place, the harder it is to get back there quickly when we need to duck in for a respite.

If you have skipped over Chapter 4, Body Basics, now is the time to read it and take physical steps to strengthen your inner resources. This is the first key to good parenting, because you cannot give much to your child unless you are in good shape yourself. Especially when your children are young, you are supplying most of the energy that keeps your family alive. And the more alive and healthy you are, the more energy you have to help your child develop his own power sources.

Time Off for Good Behavior

No matter what else you change in your life this week, plan one block of time that is totally yours. Knowing you have this time coming to you often makes it possible to get through the worst of days. If child-care responsibilities make this difficult, turn to Chapter 7 and work with your daily chart to make time available. Then ask a friend, a neighbor, a relative, or a professional child-care worker to watch your child for one afternoon or evening a week. If you can't afford this service, exchange babysitting time with a friend, or even start a chain with several friends or neighbors. If each of four mothers takes all the children for an evening or a slumber party one night a month, each could end up with three weekend evenings a month of free time.

If you don't know anyone who would like to exchange child-care services, what else do you have to barter with? Do you do crochet work, knit, sew? Could you do shopping or errands for an older woman who has no children of her own and would like to feel part of a family? Can you do light repair work, carpentry, ironing, baking? These and other skills can be bartered for child-care service.

Handling Conflict

All of us, but women especially, are taught to see conflict as something frightening and evil ... [but] in its most basic sense, conflict is inevitable, the source of all growth, and an absolute necessity if one is to be alive.

—JEAN BAKER MILLER, M.D.
Toward a New Psychology of Women

Many of us are raised to believe that conflict is a sign of failure, that things have broken down. So disagreement makes us worry and we try our best to avoid it. In doing so, we may fall into a trap of discords set up by another—an ex-husband or a teenager, for instance—in which we are bound to come out losers.

Conflict is, as Dr. Miller points out, an inevitable and necessary part of life. But while being at odds may be a negative experience (all-out battles where no one feels good and no one gains anything), it can also be positive. Positive encounters consist of honest communication where each side compromises with and respects the other. This may be hard to achieve if you have never practiced it, or when your material or emotional resources are limited. Consider, for instance, how it feels two weeks from payday when the rent is coming due, you are running out of groceries, and you don't know how you are going to pay the gas bill. In the middle of opening a can of soup you hear a little voice saying, "Mommy, why are we having soup again? I want a Big Mac and french fries, a chocolate milk-shake and . . ."

If you had enough money, you could say, "Sure, honey, let's go out for a hamburger." Or, if it had been a really trying day, you could suggest an acceptable alternative, perhaps calling out for a pizza. But being short on cash, you are tempted to reply impatiently.

Without emotional resources, it can be equally difficult to respond kindly in such a situation. By paying attention to body-mind basics you create a firmer emotional state for dealing with differences. And by learning new techniques for dealing with conflict you cut the chances of stressful open warfare. In *Toward a New Psychology of Women,* Jean Baker Miller discusses some of the ways adults can make use of situations requiring resolution. Some of her suggestions can be applied to mother-child interactions as well.

- Approach differences of opinion positively, knowing it is just as likely that you and your child will learn something valuable about yourselves as it is that you will stimulate hostility. Viewed without fear, conflict is a tool for growth. Recognizing that differences often signify a failure of communication or a need for clarification can get you off on the right foot.

- Maintain respect for your child. Being bigger and stronger, you could end discussion with a smack on the bottom. But this accomplishes little except to teach your child it isn't safe to disagree. Taking five deep breaths and sitting down can help remind you not to take advantage of your size.

- Make sure your child offers you the same courtesy. This may be difficult with young children who have not learned to control their emotions yet; and you are not going to feel like negotiating with a teen who is mouthing off at your expense. If necessary, wait until frustration levels are lower. Suggesting you and your child go to separate rooms and cool off for half an hour will be more productive. In addition,

- Don't react. Differences of opinion with your child may trigger memories of abuse you may have experienced with your parents or your ex-spouse. Remember this is a brand-new situation and that you and your child are in a different space and time. You have the power to create a learning exchange where you and your child will come out richer human beings.

- Make sure both sides of the story are fully heard. Don't assume you know what's going on in your child's head. Focus on her and look at the situation from her eyes. Then make sure she knows exactly how the matter looks from a mother's point of view.

- Strive for solutions that serve some of your needs and some of hers. Not all solutions will be perfect, and sometimes you will simply have to say no. But how you say no is very important. And if your child knows that you will usually be willing to negotiate on important matters, she won't feel driven to unreasonable outbursts born of previous frustrations.

As Miller advises, it is not conflict itself that produces violence. It is suppression of differences that creates eruptions that eat away at family unity.

PARENTING KEY NO. 2—COMMUNITY SUPPORT

All parents need help from time to time in raising their children. Sometimes parents fail to use the resources around them for all the reasons previously discussed (isolation, fear that asking will appear as failure). And some mothers fear that if they ask for help their children may be taken away from them—by the state, or by their children's father through legal procedures. So all too often mothers and their children suffer in silence, unable to make use of help that may be only a phone call away.

Overcoming a reluctance to ask for help is the first step. If you feel uncomfortable doing this, you might fortify yourself with the thought that establishing a connection with an ongoing network can eventually turn into a two-way safety line. When your resources are very limited, it can be inconceivable to think of yourself as a resource for your community. But chances are that somewhere down the line you'll find yourself paying back help when some other woman has a similar problem. This can be a great boost to self-esteem.

When Do We Need Help?

The Boston Women's Health Book Collective (BWHBC) discusses some of the kinds of help each parent needs to seek out from time to time.

- Entering situations that are new or that cause tension and stress: What is considered new and stressful varies from woman to woman so there are no hard-and-fast rules. If you are very shy, you may find it stressful to deal with persons in authority. Even setting up an appointment to talk to your child's teacher may be so uncomfortable for you that you may need a little push from a friend. Some women take encounters with others in stride, but find themselves climbing walls when they have to spend four nights alone with only their children for company.

- An accident or health problem: Accidents and illness to yourself or your child can be very frightening, or simply inconvenient. These situations often call for help from others—whether it means asking a neighbor for a ride to the hospital or asking a friend to bring you some groceries when all the kids are down with flu.

- Learning new skills: Every mother needs to learn new skills at different points in her life. These may be emotional skills in mediating sibling jealousies, or basic practical skills such as treating the measles. Often practical skills can be learned through self-education—books, magazines, hints from television, radio, or newspapers. Emotional skills, however, cannot be learned totally in isolation and require practice at interaction with others.

Once you have recognized the need for help with a particular problem, where do you turn?

For most women, help is gathered from many sources—relatives, friends, lovers, neighbors, babysitters, teachers, women's support groups, co-workers, and health professionals, to name just a few.

An ever-growing number of organizations and institutions is also available to help women with temporary or long-term needs. The BWHBC offers this list of concerned organizations which may have just the advice, information, or counseling you need:

Visiting Nurse Association provides nurses who can come to your home and help you learn about baby and child care, nutrition, and other health matters.

Planned Parenthood Federation of America provides information and services related to reproduction and health care. Each local office varies somewhat, but most provide help with concerns about sex, contraception alternatives, abortion services, and medical care. One program—proving especially helpful to parents today—teaches parents skills in communicating with children about sex. If PPFA doesn't have the information you need, ask about their listing of local community resources.

La Leche League International is a grass-roots organization that now has more than three thousand groups throughout the world. You can telephone a chapter day or night for help with problems related to nursing. Most chapters have lending libraries and run meetings on topics of interest to nursing mothers.

Parents Without Partners is a national organization designed to ease adults back into the social world after death of a spouse, divorce, or separation. Some branches of PWP may be too activity-oriented for women who would rather meet other singles quietly in informal settings. But if you are comfortable in group situations, PWP may be what you're looking for. These groups are now flourishing and provide single parents an opportunity to meet others through a variety of activities from bowling to dancing.

The National Organization for Women (*NOW*) is devoted primarily to establishing sexual equality through political action. In addition to giving women support for problems concerning illegal discrimination, your local NOW chapter will probably prove an excellent reference source on support groups for consciousness raising or a multitude of other special issues of concern to women in your community.

The Coalition for Children and Youth (formerly called the National Council of Organizations for Children and Youth) was formed to coordinate federal, state, and local agencies that serve the needs of children and youth. It runs an information service for its members and publishes a monthly newsletter.

Parents Anonymous (*PA*) is a support system to help parents deal with the problem of child abuse. There are more than eight hundred chapters in the United States and Canada where parents have the benefits of member support and professional guidance. Their toll-free number is 800-421-0353 (in California, 800-352-0386).

The American Civil Liberties Union (*ACLU*) can refer you to a lawyer if you or your child has gotten into trouble with the law and you have no one to go to for legal advice. If you cannot find a local ACLU office near you, contact the national office in New York, 212-725-1222. If it is help for your child you need, ask for the Juvenile Rights Project.

Families Anonymous, Inc., is a self-help group, begun in California, for parents whose teenagers have serious problems such as disruptive behavior or drug use. Out of this organization (now in more than thirty states) has come the parenting philosophy of "tough love" which holds a child responsible for his own life. For more information, write FA at Box 344, Torrance, California 90501.

National Clearinghouse for Drug Abuse may prove helpful if you or your teen has a drug problem. Write this office for information on specific or general questions relating to drugs, at Room 10A, 56 Parklawn Building, 5600 Fishers Lane, Rockville, Maryland 20857. One pamphlet that may prove especially helpful is "Parents, Peers and Pot."

This is only a partial list of all the organizations that may be available in your area. A check through your White Pages (begin with "parents" or "child services") will undoubtedly offer you many more. In addition, you might also want to consider local churches (some sponsor volunteer substitute-grandmother programs or "intentional families"—where you are assigned to a group of other people of varying ages, all of whom act to provide family support although separate living arrangements are maintained), your health-clinic nurse practitioner, local library, mental health center, or community bulletin boards.

Once you begin seeking the help you need, use persistence. Not all agencies are as immediately welcoming and helpful as they could be. If you write all information down, and ask each person you speak with for additional referrals, you will increase your chances for successful connections. For a more complete discussion of effective help seeking, see *Ourselves and Our Children*.

Role Models

As for me, I could live from now on without a husband. But I think the kids worry because they don't have a father. I sit down and talk with them but it's not like a father. Teddy's the one—he says he wishes his daddy would come and take him fishing.

It is impossible for you to provide your son with all that he will need to know to feel secure about himself as a boy growing toward manhood. Just as your daughter needs to know what it is like to be a woman—and learns this from you and other women—so your son needs other males to help him fashion his ideas of what he could or should become. Some fathers maintain close contact with their children after separation. If this is the case, and you believe your child's father is serving as a positive model for male behavior, you are ahead of the game. But many fathers have little or no contact with their children once a marriage is ended.

Before you panic and try to force your reluctant ex-husband

into parenting responsibilities, ask yourself whether your child's natural father is the best role model. Other men may be more suitable if your child's father lacks many of the qualities you would like to see developing in your son. Dr. Lee Salk has this advice for single mothers: "Having a father around who is weak and who does not take responsibilities with his child can sometimes be worse than having no father. After all, if someone takes the role but does not play the part adequately, it prevents someone else from filling the role and perhaps doing a better job."

Positive role models do not have to be full-time members of a family. They can be found in favorite uncles, teachers, coaches, neighbors, a minister or rabbi, a Big Brother, or friends of the family. Ideally, a role model should be someone your child likes and respects, and who accepts your child as he is, expressing affection and liking in ways that are obvious to your child.

Role models (male and female) are important to us throughout our lives, not just when we are children. But they are especially important for children at certain stages: during their early preschool years and during the preteens.

At some point between three and five years, children form temporary attachments to opposite-sex partners. If you have a son, this will present little problem. But a daughter will need some contact with a supportive male at this point. If you are not involved with a lover who can serve as a model for your child, you may want to contact a male friend of yours, an uncle, or some other man who would be willing to spend a little time with your daughter at home or on an occasional outing.

Around eight to ten years, your child will lean toward the gang and a same-sex parent. And between ten and thirteen, your child is again apt to seek out an adult of the same sex. At this point your son needs a strong male model, and his teacher, coach, a neighbor, or your lover may play an important part in his development.

Your preteen daughter may find the encouragement and acceptance she needs through a friend of yours, a Big Sister, a relative, a Sunday school teacher, the mother of her best friend, or one of your co-workers. (You may hear one day, "I'm going to be just like Aunt Sally when I grow up!" Aunt Sally works for an airline and appears very glamorous to an eleven-year-old.) If you are aware of this stage of your daughter's development, you will not be taken unaware or needlessly hurt. You will be able to deal more generously with your daughter as you handle the occasional pang of jealousy and rejection you may feel.

PARENTING KEY NO. 3—EDUCATION

By extending your support networks you will automatically find you are becoming more knowledgeable about many parenting issues. Sometimes informal discussions with other mothers will provide just the play group, after-school program, or health practitioner you were looking for.

But none of us can look to others for all problem solving. Most of the work of parenting will be done by you—in the wee hours of the morning when you try to figure out why your son is suddenly so withdrawn, or over dinner when you search for something to say to your daughter to relieve her anxiety over her too quickly or too slowly developing breasts. The most effective thing you can do as a parent is to become your own best reference source.

Without some idea of how children normally develop and what they are experiencing at different stages of their development, it is all too easy to find yourself in one of these situations:

"When Sara turned two, it was no to everything. I thought she was going to be a little troublemaker all her life and I really got on her case." Had this mother realized that an inevitable part of the two-year-old's development is discovering her own identity and separateness from mother, she could have made a game of the noes with her daughter, instead of despairing that this behavior would be permanent.

"John had really gotten along with his sisters beautifully. In fact, I thought for a while, 'Well, that wasn't so hard to do. He's really going to be a nonsexist male when he grows up.' But I spoke too soon, because he just stopped having anything to do with girls. So for a while I worried that something was going really wrong, that maybe he would even end up gay." This mother would have been saved worry had she known that one day, no matter what she taught John about treating girls with respect, he would need the companionship of male peers to strengthen his identity as a nine-year-old boy.

"When my daughter started criticizing me I nearly put her through a wall. She started telling me my dresses were too short, my shoes didn't match my purse, and everything I did was sappy." Many mothers are surprised, hurt, and angered when teenagers begin to break away. Although this process doesn't have to mean years of daily confrontation, it seldom happens smoothly. Often the only way an insecure teen can begin this process is by attempting to pare her godlike parent down to size. Knowing this phase is normal, and that it doesn't last forever, helps parents cope with a lot less stress, misunderstanding, and anger.

These few examples illustrate that being a forewarned parent is being forearmed—with information that can prevent needless negative conflicts with your child. References for this chapter can provide you with more detailed information about whatever stage of development your child is now in, as well as letting you know what you can expect in the future. Texts, however, are not hard and fast; they can provide you with guidelines, but each child is an individual and will pass through the stages a little earlier or later than another one.

FEW SIMPLE ANSWERS

It can be tempting to look for simple answers to problems you may be having with your child. And sometimes, if a problem has not been let go too long, simple answers exist. But often emotional difficulties haven't sprung up overnight. The symptoms you see in your child may be expressions of inner difficulties s/he has been wrestling with for months or years.

How long a problem has gone on may determine how long it takes to do the repair work necessary to get your child back on course. If problems go uncorrected, a child may carry an unnecessary emotional burden into adulthood.

According to Dr. Lee Salk, patients whose illnesses can be attributed mainly to imbalances of the mind fill half the hospital beds in the United States. Many of these individuals are victims of foreign wars. Many others came out the losers in battlegrounds of their own homes.

Because children are easier to return to health than adults, prevention of emotional problems should be every parent's goal. Parents may disagree drastically on how to accomplish this goal. Even child psychologists disagree on some of the solutions to questions such as when to show unconditional love and when to discipline children. The guidelines offered here are attempts to synthesize the best advice being offered by professionals and parents. These will have to be modified, of course, by your own intuition.

- All behavior is caused. Children "act out" for a reason. Unusually disruptive behavior is a sure sign something uncomfortable is going on inside. In this case, you should investigate, not punish.

- Your child will be healthier if you continually add to self-esteem by making sure s/he feels loved (not overly indulged or overprotected) and worthwhile. Do you hug your child, and explain that you love him or her whether or not s/he wins or loses? Do you applaud the things s/he does well? And do you give your child room for occasional failure, without fear of your displeasure?

- Some combination of your needs and your child's needs must be met to successfully resolve conflicts between you. This means being a real person with your child, one who is not afraid to set limits when necessary, but who respects her child's sense of privacy and personal dignity.

It is hard to deal with issues that are not clearly stated. But often children are unable to discuss their problems. Perhaps a child feels unsafe telling a parent what is wrong because there is no bond of trust. Or a child may be only partially aware of the problem until it is aired. Even if a child can express what is wrong, his real needs may be completely misinterpreted by an adult who is only half listening.

LEARNING TO LISTEN

Being a good listener is a difficult talent to develop. Many parents are so anxious to teach and shape their children that they are always looking for a way to take the lead. Often what is needed is to take a more passive, accepting role: to have faith in your child's ability to work a problem through on his own once he has sounded it out.

Even very young children can be ingenious at problem solving—once they are allowed to own the problem and take responsibility for creating its outcome and living with its consequences. Being allowed to solve problems also increases a child's ability to think, and adds to self-esteem. This may be easier to see if you think about how you would feel if all decisions were made for you, before you had time to come up with some possibilities on your own. Thomas Gordon (*Parent Effectiveness Training*) has some suggestions for parents who want to learn more workable listening and responding techniques.

- Whenever possible, focus full attention on your child, especially when you become aware that your child has a special need to communicate. It will be difficult for your child to believe you are all there while you are giving half an ear to the television or cutting up stew meat.

- Practice nonjudgmental responses, the same kind you would give to a good friend. Simply listen for a while sometimes, and empathize with your child's feelings. Suppose, for instance, your five-year-old came running in to you screaming, "I hate Karen! I hate her. I hate her." Her best friend has just broken off her doll's head, the doll she has been toting around since she was two. What do you say? ("Now darling, it's all right. Mommy will get you another doll tomorrow." "Judy! You don't really mean that.

I can fix your doll and I'm sure Karen didn't mean to break it."
"What an awful thing to say. It's only a doll. You go right back
out there and apologize to Karen.") Gordon suggests that the majority of responses that immediately come to mind would be ones
that indicate you are not really hearing your child's pain. And
sometimes what children most want and need is to know that you
understand how awful the world looks to them in some moments.
Once they are assured you understand, strong emotions don't
have to stay trapped inside, and children can return to equilib-
rium more smoothly.

Often parents have difficulty accepting their children's strong
emotions because they themselves were never allowed the same
courtesy. So it can be very frightening when your angelic daughter turns into a red-faced, earsplitting, outraged demon. It can
help then to remember that emotions are very transitory—if they
are released. Most children will go from hate to tears to sullen-
ness to smiles again very quickly, if they feel they have been understood. In the case mentioned above, Judy was perfectly
justified in feeling momentary hatred toward her friend. And a
response from her mother that said "Oh, how angry you must feel
right now" (and perhaps the offer of a pillow-substitute to sock
around for a while) would let Judy own her feelings and get them
out safely. But if she were made to apologize (or were talked
down to) for feeling so angry, how would she feel? It is likely she
would feel the same way a very angry adult would—even worse
than she did before she opened her mouth.

This does not mean that children should be allowed to go on
tears through the house or sock other little children. There is a
difference between permitting expression of *feelings* and permitting negative *actions*.

- Try, as much as possible, to eliminate name-calling from your interactions. Gordon explains that this can be facilitated by practicing "I-statements" rather than "you-statements." Say what *you*
are feeling rather than hurling accusations at your child. Imagine,
for instance, someone saying to you, "You are a real slob." What
does that do to your self-esteem? And what does it do to your
level of resistance to further communication? When we are called
names and labeled, we are tempted to call names back, and to put
up our defenses and stop listening. The same applies to children.

Also, name-calling is a less direct form of communication. And when you are parenting, you need all the directness you can get to prevent misinterpreted messages. For instance, if you say to your teenager, "I am really tired of the clothes all over the floor in your room. I'm embarrassed when my friends come over and have to pass your door on the way to the bathroom," your message is very clear. And you may be able to find a negotiation point. By yelling, "Your room is a pigsty! Why don't you do something about it?," you are just setting yourself up for one more sullen go-round.

NEED FOR NEGOTIATION

To meet the needs that both of you have for respect, dignity, and happiness, negotiation with your child is often in order. Learning to negotiate is an art, and like listening, it is not the easiest talent to develop. But it can be learned through trial and error. If communication with your child has broken down completely, you may want to seek informal or professional advice from support groups or parenting classes. But if communication lines are only temporarily disconnected, you will find it helpful to adopt some of the techniques developed by Gordon for PET courses. Most any parent-child relationship can benefit when you remember these tips.

- When a conflict arises, don't let it get pushed under the rug. Establish a time convenient for both you and your child to discuss it—not while you're in the middle of making a cheese sauce, or when your child is half asleep.

- In advance, set guidelines such as no name-calling and reasonable levels of sound, and agree that both sides will be fully heard and that you are going to work through to a solution that will be acceptable to both of you.

- Allow your child to go first and to name the problem, using "I-statements," not "you-statements." Repeat the problem as you see it and make sure you are both in agreement about what the problem is.

- Ask your child to come up with as many possible solutions as s/he can. However improbable they may seem to you, list them all without judgment or comment on a large sheet of paper. Then list all possible solutions you feel you could live with, again taking the needs of both of you into consideration. Often, if a child is aware that s/he can participate in negotiation and that the solution is one s/he will have to live with, a child can be very adept at problem solving.

- Slowly eliminate all but the most likely candidates, until you are left with the solution that meets the most needs and which gives you both a reasonable assurance of its workability.

- Agree to try the compromise for a while and to check in periodically with each other to see how the solution is meeting each person's needs. Sometimes what looks workable will turn out— through no deliberate fault on anyone's part—not to be. You may find, for example, that you've been asked to handle an important, ongoing social responsibility during the hour you agreed to spend a little more playtime with your son. Or it may turn out that your son's basketball practice has been changed to the hour he agreed to spend each afternoon helping you with housework. In either case, as in others, renegotiation will have to take place.

This kind of democratic approach can work for many kinds of parent-child conflicts, but will be unworkable for others. In the long run, home democracy may often save you repetitious attempts to force a child to change his behavior entirely. When well handled, it is usually less hostile than parent-directed solutions to problems, allows your child to take more responsibility for handling his life, and makes mothers feel much less like frustrated ogresses. (For detailed accounts of how this "no-lose" technique can work, and for information on what may be happening when it doesn't appear to be working for your family, see *Parent Effectiveness Training* or *P.E.T. in Action* by Thomas Gordon.)

If you are interested in radically altering your parenting style, there is nothing like another group of parents to give you ongoing information and support. Locate a group by contacting one or more of the sources listed earlier in this chapter.

THE PROBLEM CHILD

Jerry was a problem from the day he was born.

We have all seen children who seem to give their mothers headaches wherever they go. Their behavior is unacceptable to most adults, they don't respond to reason or affection, and they often seem to hate the world. Research in the last twenty years is helping show how such antisocial behavior may be linked to abnormalities of the body. But often this kind of behavior results from early childhood experiences. Before we examine some of the possible physiological causes of problem behavior, let's look at some of the ways family or school influences can contribute to imbalance. Lee Salk (*What Every Child Would Like His Parents to Know*) suggests misbehavior is likely to occur:

- If a child has never experienced early gratification of his or her needs for unconditional love, warmth and closeness, sucking as well as simply feeding, touching, gentleness, and habitual cleanliness;
- If a child has experienced a series of events that encouraged misbehavior, such as a teacher or parent who responded only when a child acted out;
- If a child's actions were always punished, regardless of whether his actions were positive or negative. In such a case, a child will be unable to tell right from wrong.

Sometimes, however, there seems to be no apparent reason for problem behavior. Some children appear to have been born hyperactive and overly aggressive, and this indeed may be the case. A recent article in *Science Digest* ("Brain Triggers: Biochemistry and Behavior" by Joann Ellison Rodgers) documents the work now being done to explain how physical abnormalities can cause emotional disturbances in children (and adults).

If you have a problem child, this article is worth exploring once you have ruled out emotional causes. Biochemical imbalances are suspected of contributing to some cases of hyperactivity, depression, aggressive, violent, and impulsive behavior, schizophrenia, and autism, according to Rodgers.

Some parents may be familiar with Tourette's syndrome. Victims, most often boys, develop twitches, may move in a jerky fashion, and may display outbursts of obscenity and hostile gestures. This disease has a genetic base, and milder forms of similar behavior may be related to Tourette's syndrome. Rodgers reports that drug therapies are being developed to treat Tourette's and DeLange syndrome (DeLange children are withdrawn and "uncuddly," may posture with hands in certain patterns, and are prone to self-mutilation and rocking movements).

Extremes in behavior are also being linked to causes such as fetal-alcohol-syndrome, niacin deficiency, abnormal amounts of copper and zinc, and even to the chemicals found in sodas and other processed foods children consume. (This very important issue of diet and behavior is discussed further in Chapter 5.) If you have tried psychotherapy without results and/or believe your child's behavior may have a physiological base, you may want to explore diet modification or other treatments now available with an informed and empathetic physician. While some doctors are prone to view behavioral problems as almost always parent-caused, others take a more holistic approach. Check your network thoroughly for the names of doctors your friends have found most helpful.

A NOTE ON CHILDREN WITH SPECIAL NEEDS

Each year unknown numbers of schoolchildren are incorrectly evaluated by teachers as "slow learners" and treated as if they were intellectually impaired. As many as one out of every ten children may be affected by learning disabilities—"disorders of listening, thinking, talking, reading, writing, spelling, or arithmetic."[1] These children are not mentally retarded. They have perceptual problems.

One such problem is a condition called dyslexia. A child with dyslexia finds reading and writing extremely difficult because numbers and letters in texts or on the blackboard may appear very different to him than to most people. He may see them backward, sideways, or as any of a variety of scribbles or squiggles.

Dyslexia is a perceptual problem because a child simply cannot see letters and numbers in the ordinary way; it is not an intellectual deficiency. And it is often very difficult for a parent or a teacher to detect, especially once a child has been labeled a slow learner. A bright child sometimes learns to compensate on her own, by translating what she sees into what she is expected to see. This is a painstaking mental effort, however, especially difficult if a child is stressed or tired, and it cannot be accomplished quickly in any case. (Parents should also be aware that some school districts may not be eager to diagnose and inform parents of this and other learning disabilities if they are required by law to provide expensive supplemental teaching programs for children with these problems.)

If you suspect your child may be dyslectic, ask him or her to copy *very quickly* some rows of words or number combinations; results may appear as squiggles with a few correctly copied letters mixed in. In this case you should ask your librarian for a book explaining dyslexia. If your child seems to have symptoms of dyslexia, have her or him tested for the disorder and seek special reading help through your local school. It is, unfortunately, up to you to pursue solutions, because often those who should be aware of this problem are not. One woman was repeatedly reassured by her pediatrician that her child simply had "emotional difficulties" and it was not until two years later that she finally discovered her daughter had dyslexia. (For more information on learning disabilities, see *Your Child Can Win* by Joan Noyes and Norma Macneill. This excellent reference provides parents with strategies, activities, and games they can employ with the learning-disabled child.)

Problems with impaired vision can also cause a child to be incorrectly labeled as mentally retarded. The National Society to Prevent Blindness advocates preschool screening (examinations and tests to determine the level of a child's visual acuity). Many nearsighted children, for example, suffer needlessly, simply for want of an adequate diagnosis. If you believe your child may have eye problems rather than intellectual disabilities, contact this organization at 79 Madison Avenue, New York, New York 10016, and ask what can be done. There are spin-off groups that may be available locally, such as the Pittsburgh Blind Association, which provides instructions to parents interested in initiating preschool screening for children between the ages of three and six.

FACTS AND FANTASY

The books your child reads, in school and at home, can have a strong influence on his life. They provide him with facts he needs to know, encourage independent problem solving, extend his view of the world beyond his city streets, and can even help him deal with emotional difficulties that he may be unable to talk about.

Modern books for children often take the direct approach to education and problem solving. They can be helpful in offering straightforward advice about specific concerns, such as how to make sense of death, divorce, or sexuality. Fantasy can show a child that it is possible to handle strong, conflicting emotions (more of this later).

Your child is likely to use books as tools if:

- Books are readily available at home;
- Books are a routine part of your own life;
- You encourage trips to the library (some libraries offer special activities for children, such as story times, which could provide a fun outing for you and your child, to learn and to meet new and interesting people);
- You are willing to devote some portion of your week to reading stories and/or helping him master words that may be a bit beyond his grasp.

With a little imagination, you can create word games that encourage exploration of books of fact and fiction, including dictionaries or encyclopedias. You might try a reward system, such as awarding praise and/or a penny for every word he discovers that you can't define. Rainy, indoor play days can be turned into enjoyable sharing times by encouraging your child to make up lists of ten related items (ten animals; ten kinds of trees, etc.).

Your child may get into the spirit of exploration faster if he feels he can teach you sometimes too, so don't be afraid to admit, "Gee, I didn't know that. That's really interesting. I'm glad you found that out."

Including at least one book as a gift for birthdays and special holidays will give your child a head start in his education for adulthood. Be sure to include topics of interest to him—not just to you. And books should be those written for his appropriate reading level, neither too easy nor so difficult that reading becomes a chore. Check with your child's teacher or librarian if you have any questions.

Fairy tales are often overlooked by parents of the *Sesame Street* generation. But child psychologist Bruno Bettelheim (*The Uses of Enchantment*) believes a book of these tales may be one of the best investments you could make in your child's emotional development. Finding meaning in our lives, Bettelheim points out, is a difficult and ongoing task. To do so, it is necessary that we:

- Have hope for the future;
- Believe in our ability to master life;
- Develop a sense of morality to help us live well with others and make a personal contribution to society.

Fairy tales, Bettelheim feels, provide an ideal means of helping a child achieve these goals. While fairy tales do not deal with the objects of our modern culture (computers, economic reports, calculus, or inflation) they *can* help a child derive meaning from his world and enrich his inner life. How do they do this?

- Fairy tales state existential problems briefly and simply, at a level a child can understand.

- They help a child understand that much of what goes wrong in life has to do with our dual natures. (Modern stories may be sugarcoated, with "good" characters only. But children are aware that they are not always good. So if all humans are supposed to be good, but the child is not, he feels he must be a monster.) Fairy tales let a child know life is a struggle with our generous intentions and our selfish ones, but that he can conquer his "evil" side in the end.

- Fairy tales can help the child in a split home deal with loss and change. Often tales begin with the death of a mother or father, and move on to show a child he can come out all right even so.

- These tales can help a child develop a sense of right and wrong— by identifying with heroes and heroines and reading about the punishment meted out in the end to evil characters.

- And fairy tales teach that finding adult love can help us overcome fears of death and separation, that grasping onto our parents does not provide the answer to our fears.

Many parents find that some combination of modern stories and older tales provide children with a more balanced literary diet. Younger children may love the nonsensical, repetitive rhythms of Mother Goose or Dr. Seuss. But almost any child will enjoy a good adventure story told in simple but colorful language. Whether they are fairy tales, classics, or other stories, Bettelheim offers some cautionary advice for reading stories with your child.

- Pay attention to your child's response. S/he will indicate which ones are most useful by immediate reactions or by asking to hear the story again.

- Allow your child to choose which story s/he finds particularly helpful at each stage of development. It is best to follow your child's lead.

- If you guess why a particular story has such appeal for your child, keep the information to yourself. Children need to know they can keep their thoughts secret until they choose to reveal them to you.

And sometimes a child may be unaware of why a story is so appealing. By explaining what it is that so delights, you may take away the enchantment.

TELEVISION PROS AND CONS

In many homes the television set is on a lot more than it is off. For some mothers, programs serve to lessen the sense of isolation, to provide information, and to act as a home babysitter and amusement center. Often parents are unaware of the enormous impact television has on the home except for obvious conflicts over who can watch what program when. While television serves many useful functions, like anything else, it can be overdone. Some children may even become TV abusers, seeking out the tube to the exclusion of homework, friends, or outside activities. (The advent of video games has probably cut down the average child's passive viewing time but creates its own set of problems.)

Television serves as a teacher for your child, giving him continual information about what the world is all about. But what kind of a teacher is it?

Programs project values that you may not hold and might not want your child to acquire. And television does not always reflect an accurate view of life. Recent studies from the Media Institute in Washington, D.C., indicate just how slanted television's view of crime is, for example. Five of the most serious kinds of crime—murder, rape, kidnapping, aggravated assault, and robbery—make up the majority (88 percent) of crimes depicted on television. Yet these crimes account for less than 8 percent of the actual crimes reported by the FBI in 1980.[2] How does this affect the average television viewer? Could it give us a view of the world that is more hostile and frightening than reality?

A minority of parents have decided that the cons of television are not outweighed by the pros; they opt for other forms of home entertainment. Many parents, however, create solutions by confining television viewing to particular programs or to the publicly funded channels. Whatever approach you take to television in your home, here are two of the reasons it can make parenting tougher.

- Young children are gullible and literal. Research shows that young children cannot distinguish between commercials and regular programs; what they see on the screen is reality to them. This can lead to very distorted impressions. And programs which are far beyond a child's emotional capacity to handle can lead to mixed anxieties or nightmares.

- Commercials program children to crave junk foods as well as many useless, expensive, or overrated toys. This can create numerous hassles for you on trips to the supermarket and in demands for expensive merchandise.

It is unlikely you would feed your child cupcakes three meals a day, or buy your six-year-old pornography or books filled with colored pictures of violent deaths and dismemberments. The same discretion should be applied to what goes into your child's mind through the television set.

Source Notes
1. Joan Noyes and Norma Macneill, *Your Child Can Win* (New York: William Morrow, 1982), p. 7.
2. Michael Himowitz, "TV crime more violent than crime on streets," Daily Magazine, *Pittsburgh Post-Gazette,* January 13, 1982, p. 17.

References
Adams, Jane. *Sex and the Single Parent.* New York: Coward, McCann & Geoghegan, 1978.
Bernard, Jessie. *The Future of Motherhood.* New York: Penguin, 1975.
Bettelheim, Bruno. *The Uses of Enchantment.* New York: Alfred Knopf, 1976.
Bonham, Marilyn. *The Laughter and Tears of Children.* New York: Macmillan, 1968.
Boston Women's Health Book Collective. *Ourselves and Our Children.**
New York: Random House, 1978.

* Recommended reading

Briggs, Dorothy Corkville. *Your Child's Self-Esteem.** New York: Doubleday, 1975.

Gesell, Arnold, and Frances Ilg. *Infant and Child in the Culture of Today.* New York: Harper & Row, 1943. (Somewhat dated but contains valuable detailed descriptions of stages of children's development.)

Gesell, Arnold, and Frances Ilg. *The Child from Five to Ten.* New York: Harper & Row, 1946.

Gesell, Arnold, et al. *Youth: The Years from Ten to Sixteen.* New York: Harper & Row, 1956.

Gordon, Thomas. *Parent Effectiveness Training.* New York: Wyden, 1970.

Gordon, Thomas, and Judith Gordon Sands. *P.E.T. in Action.* New York: Wyden, 1976.

LeShan, Eda. *How to Survive Parenthood.* New York: Random House, 1965.

Miller, Jean Baker. *Toward a New Psychology of Women.* Beacon Press, Boston, 1976.

Noyes, Joan, and Norma Macneill. *Your Child Can Win.* New York: William Morrow, 1982.

Rodgers, Joann. "Brain Triggers: Biochemistry and Behavior," *Science Digest,* Vol. 91, No. 1, p. 60 ff.

Salk, Lee. *What Every Child Would Like His Parents to Know.* New York: David McKay, 1972.

* Recommended reading

CHAPTER NINE

Day Care: The Great Debate

How can I afford to work? Half my paycheck would go for day care.

Working mothers everywhere are now dealing with an issue that has reached the point of national debate. Day care. How do you find someone you can trust to care for your children while you work? And how can you afford to pay for it? When is it "safe" to leave your child and what effects will your absence have on his or her development?

As more single mothers enter the work force they are faced with questions that often have no easy solutions. The need for resolution of day-care options for working mothers is becoming increasingly apparent. Yet government and private industry have, so far, offered few productive alternatives compared to Europe, the Soviet Union, and Japan. Options are severely limited for the single working mother in America, and are likely to remain so for some time. Married couples can, if necessary, arrange split-shift jobs and child-care routines. But this choice is not one a single mother can make.

The general availability of flextime work schedules or on-site nurseries would allow working mothers more time to spend with young children while earning a living. Arranging for some full-time jobs to be handled by two half-time workers would also be a step in the right direction. Some employers do agree to this arrangement when approached; few offer this as a standard option. Not only can it work well for employees, it can actually save money for employers who do not have to provide expensive benefits to a full-time worker. If you know another single mother interested in a half-time job, this alternative may be worth pursuing. Some women have even been able to bring an infant or young child to the workplace. But this solution is available only to a small percentage of women with a typical work situation. Most of these options are not available to the majority of working women.

So most mothers are left on their own to handle decisions about the day-care dilemma. These issues are not made easier for women who are bombarded with criticism as they attempt to juggle work or school with mothering responsibilities.

GUILT TRIPPERS

It is hard enough to deal with personal feelings of guilt the first day you leave your child with a day-care worker. What you don't need to hear are putdowns from others:

My ex-husband came over today and said I'm ignoring the kids because of my school. I feel like he's waiting for me to quit or flunk.

My neighbor tries to make me feel awful. She says, 'Mothers should be home with their kids. Working mothers cause juvenile delinquency.'

My ex-husband gives me a lot of guilt about the kids. He really makes my situation worse. He says, 'You're destroying the kids by working.'

Women are in a no-win situation. If they stay home with their children the family doesn't eat; if they go to work they are told they aren't being good mothers. Someone out there is just waiting to tell you that you are going to end up raising neglected children who will soon be making the drug scene or mugging little old women. As one woman said, "Society makes you feel like you should be there all the time for your kids. They make you feel so guilty you forget about all the mothers who sit home with their kids and are closet drinkers or simply fail to communicate with their children."

The next time you are confronted with a guilt tripper, it might be helpful to keep in mind a few facts and one big fiction.

Fiction

• If a mother works her children are apt to be insecure and deprived.

Fact

• Children of at-home mothers are no happier than the children of working mothers.

• Children need some routine undivided attention from parents (the minimum amount will vary with age). But the quality of time you spend with your child is more important than the quantity. And quality can be improved if you are with your child when you want to be, not because you feel you have to be.

• Child care can improve your mental health. Women interviewed by Stress and Families who had adequate child-care assistance—during normal times and for emergencies—experienced better mental health according to all five indicators used. The more help a woman had available, the more control she felt she exercised over her life, and the better her self-esteem. These positive feelings are reflected in children's feelings of well-being.

• Children of working mothers often develop certain social skills at an earlier age, and these may aid their sense of independence and self-reliance.

- The quickest way for your child to feel deprived is by not having food on the table. Try to remember this next time you have to delay dinner because of your job, or are guilt-tripped about not being home twenty-four hours a day.

WHAT MAKES THE DIFFERENCE?

Research indicates that the children of working mothers are not less happy or well adjusted simply because their mothers work. This finding reaffirms what some mothers have already found out. Children are resilient and very adaptable. They can deal with many changes, as long as they are reassured of their mother's love and are made to feel secure in new routines.

What makes a difference is not the number of hours you spend with your child, but how you and your child feel about that time. This isn't to say that many children wouldn't prefer that Mom were at home twenty-four hours a day to see to each whim and keep the cookie jar filled. But children would also rather play Atari than do their homework. Children are children, not adults. And only you can determine what is best for the whole family.

Few single mothers have ideal work and day-care situations. But if you are about to return to work, things are likely to go more smoothly if:

- You are confident about your decision to work and firmly express it to your child—without apologies:
- You are getting some personal satisfaction (and reasonable pay) from your job and are not feeling too overloaded by double responsibilities;
- You are confident about your day-care worker;
- You have an established routine which allows your child a reassuring amount of time with you each day or evening.

Most single mothers could use more time, more money, or both. But just because you work doesn't mean your children will have to feel less happy. In fact, it's very possible everyone will end up benefiting.

HOW WILL YOUR CHILD'S BEHAVIOR CHANGE?

Your child's behavior may alter to adjust to your nine to five schedule. Any mother who has left her child with a babysitter or a day-care worker knows that the first temporary partings are seldom accomplished smoothly. Children need reassurance that you are not leaving forever—especially if they have experienced the loss, in one way or another, of their father.

Moments of anxiety are normal—especially at first, as your child adjusts to being on his or her own without you. But with other children around, your child will soon become absorbed in new faces and experiences.

Once your child adjusts, you may notice positive changes, such as copying your more independent behavior. These are some of the things mothers most often notice once their children are in day care:

More extroverted behavior. "Sharon got used to it very quickly, I think it was healthy for her. It made her an easygoing child, and very outgoing."

An earlier sense of independence. "Kids of working parents really rely on themselves and use their wits. They have to deal with other kids, with other people, not just parents. They learn to accept reality, not being doted on by their mothers all the time."

An increased sense of self-esteem. "She's proud to be able to take care of herself now."

In addition, some women enjoy the bonus of improved quality of time with their children. "I'm in a better mood when I'm with the kids because of having time off to be with other adults. I'm more loving with them. Of course they respond to that."

DELINQUENTS OR DOLLARS?

Still, will your need for dollars turn your children into delinquents? What about the teenage years? Won't teenagers all "get into trouble" before you get home at five-thirty?

It has been suggested that the teenage years are a trying time for a mother to be away from the home—just when the kids are having their identity crises. This is, indeed, a difficult time for children, and if you have just recently returned to work, there is little question but that your children may resent their loss of time with you.

But working does not mean desertion. And even the children of at-home mothers usually go through difficult growing experiences in their teens. Ironically, of the women interviewed by the Stress and Families Project, one who was most adamant about the negative effects on children of "coming home to an empty house" was a married woman who was at home all day. She had a host of problems with her children, including one child who was being treated for emotional problems, another arrested for shoplifting, and a third in court on charges of vandalism.

So kids will probably have growth problems whether or not you are there twenty-four hours a day to watch. Children who "act out" come from all kinds of homes: from wealthy ones as well as poor ones, from homes where parents work and where they don't work. You will have to follow your own instincts in assuring adequate communication that will alert you to any emerging problems.

THE IMPORTANCE OF ATTITUDE

Indications are that how a mother really feels about herself and her work is very important. The mother who receives some positive feedback about herself through a working experience is more likely to pass on her sense of security and happiness to her children.

Of course, if you have a job you hate and don't want to go to each day, you are probably feeling you have less love to spread around. So it pays, for everybody, if you find a job that gives you personal satisfaction in some way, and, preferably, provides you with a reasonably secure income.

If you are happy doing what you are doing, it will also help you provide the firm and nonapologetic attitude your children need to see in you. If your children sense that you are unsure about your actions, it is reasonable to assume they may begin to question, nag, or throw tantrums to try to get you to alter your course. It may be difficult to project a confidence you are not always feeling. But firmness and reassurance are important when you are establishing a new routine. Make sure your children know what the guidelines are. Understanding your child's fears can help.

> I just reasoned with her. I explained to her that life was tough and I had to go to work. She screamed on the floor but I had to go and I left. Before I left I told her it was all OK. I knew how she felt, she was mad (because she was afraid) and I was sorry, but I would be back. I tried to make sure she understood I *would* be back. And she adjusted surprisingly fast.

Here are some additional tips about attitude and approach to child care from Jean Curtis, author of *A Guide for Working Mothers.*

- Though advertisements tend to romanticize mother-child togetherness, few mothers are in a constant state of bliss simply because they are surrounded by their children.
- If you are utilizing a day-care program or some other form of child care, consistency is very important. Be there at the same time each day for pickup whenever possible, so that your child knows what his set routine is. If you are unavoidably detained, make sure you call to let your child and worker know ahead of time.
- While your child would probably prefer to be with you around the clock, she would also prefer ice cream to vegetables. The real-

ity is we can't have everything we want. And it probably wouldn't be good for us if we were able to fulfill all wishes.

- The least disruptive times to return to work are when a child is in his infancy or once he begins elementary school and no longer requires so much of your attention.

- If you have put off thoughts of work because you think it will be easier in the teen years, be aware that adolescents as well as preschoolers seem to be easily affected by sudden changes in their mothers' patterns.

Of course your situation is unique to some extent, and the smoothness of your day will depend on:

- Feelings of acceptance or resentment about the need to work;
- The degree of satisfaction with your job;
- The amount you can afford to pay for child-care arrangements;
- The number and ages of your children.

You cannot control every event relating to your child's care, and it's likely your sitter will not resemble Mary Poppins. Women are faced with a limited number of options and must choose the best of what is available and what they can reasonably afford.

OPTIONS: WHO WATCHES THE KIDS?

Finding reliable child care is essential if you are to work. Once in your job, you'll be free to do your best only if you keep worry about things at home to a minimum.

Yet finding good child care is not easy. Lucia Bequaert (*Single Women: Alone and Together*) cites the fact that more than nine million children of single parents and all together more than twenty-six million children have working mothers. Yet there are only about 905,000 spaces for children in licensed care centers.

The difficulty of finding a satisfactory child-care worker is compounded if your financial resources are scarce. Bequaert reports that only 3 percent of the available space in licensed centers accommodates children from welfare families.

Considering these limitations, working mothers have had to use a number of different approaches to child care. There is no right or wrong solution. Given your child's particular needs and what you can fit into your budget, you may end up choosing any of the following options:

Grandmothers and other relatives. A large number of single mothers find the extended family provides the answer. Often relatives come to the rescue when other options are unavailable. They may charge a nominal amount, or provide services free or on a barter basis (your time in running errands or helping with food shopping or home repairs). If you choose this option do make sure bargaining arrangements are clearly spelled out.

Day-care centers. Centers offer full-time and part-time services and are usually licensed by the state according to minimal standards of staff qualifications, safety, and health. If you are looking for a center near you, be aware that a license does not automatically mean the best available care, but check to see if the center you are interested in has met state requirements.

Family day care. Provides child care in a private home. Usually one adult cares for up to six children at a time. Providers may be legally required to register with a state or local child-care office.

Cooperative nurseries. These are informal arrangements which may be made by you and a group of other women. If you know other working mothers who are also looking for child care, this might be an answer for all of you. Play groups usually operate in families' homes. You may get together to pool resources and hire one worker, or the group may decide to share the responsibility, each woman providing an agreed-upon amount of time each week.

Nursery schools. These offer part-time programs which usually operate for three or four hours a day. Sometimes they offer morning or afternoon programs.

Private babysitters. You may find a sitter who will come to your home, or you may take your child to the home of a local sitter. Sitters often work for very reasonable fees, especially if they are students or women who are not interested in work outside the home. But babysitting fees are now covered under minimum wage laws if you require more than twenty hours a week. So some sitters may request the current minimum wage rate of $3.35 an hour.

After-school/extended-day programs. These may be available for your school-aged child if you work past the regular school hours. Check with your child's school for information. And be aware that schools may be a good source of potential help if you have had no luck finding a worker through other channels. The mothers of your children's friends, or others you may meet through school programs or PTA, may be interested in starting up a child-care service in their homes.

If you have a child-care clearinghouse in your area, it can give you the most thorough information about what is available to you. If not, you will have to try the yellow pages, word of mouth, women's centers, bulletin boards in laundromats and supermarkets, or social services.

WHAT TO LOOK FOR

Much of the following information on child-care-facility screening and financing, including the sample family day-care contract, has been supplied by the Child Care Resource Center (CRC) in Cambridge, Massachusetts. This organization has been of aid to thousands of mothers in the last decade and welcomes inquiries of all kinds relating to child-care alternatives.

Bear in mind that these are suggestions for finding *optimal* care. But few single mothers find exactly what they want and many even find affordable care difficult to come by. It is likely you will have to compromise on some things. But here are some guidelines to keep in mind.

- Plan ahead whenever possible. If you are interested in a center, you may need to find one and to register four to six months before you will actually need it. Begin looking for family day care at least a month or two ahead of time.

- Make notes or discuss with staff your concerns in the areas of:

  —the staff-children relationship;
  —health, safety, physical space;
  —parent involvement;
  —the program/activities that are provided and values being taught.

- If you have time, plan to visit more than one center or home, even if you like the first provider you find. The more you visit, the more comfortable you will feel with your final choice.

- Allow enough time for visits. For day-care centers, CRC recommends you call in advance and arrange about a half-hour interview with its director, ten to fifteen minutes with potential teachers, and an hour for observing. Family day-care visits should allow an hour to an hour and a half, preferably when other children are present so you can see how things operate.

Are You Happy with the Staff?

The most important part of any program is its staff. The most spacious setting and wonderful toys will not make up for a man or woman you don't feel comfortable with. So carefully consider the qualities of anyone you think about hiring. These following suggestions are the result of research at the Child Development Unit of Children's Hospital in Boston.

- If you can, be there during arrival time to see how the provider and parents relate. How does the staff handle a child who may be upset at her parent's departure?

- Are children relaxed during meal or snack times? Ask whether snacks and meals are included in the fee. Are these nutritious? Be sure to discuss any food (or other) allergies your child may have.

- What about indoor activities? Does each child get some special, individual attention? Is there a balance between free and structured time?

- What about discipline? What do providers view as problem behavior? How do they draw out quiet children or handle too aggressive behavior? Are incidents handled satisfactorily from the children's point of view? Do you and the staff basically agree on how situations should be handled and on questions of physical punishment?
- Is there active group play? Does the staff encourage jumping and running or other play that will let off steam? Is there a playground, park, or yard area nearby and do children have space to be active indoors in bad weather?
- Do providers genuinely enjoy being with young children, listen to them, and remain sensitive to their needs?

Health, Safety and Physical Space
Again, these are standards for the ideal arrangement. Consider what is most important to you.

- Is the environment generally "child-proof"? Are rooms free of sharp objects and small, swallowable items. Is equipment in stable condition, and are poisons, paints, and medicines out of reach?
- Are there two exits available and a fire extinguisher?
- Are food preparation areas and bathrooms clean?
- Is there a first-aid kit handy? Do providers have any first-aid training?
- What are plans for emergencies? Phone numbers for police, fire department, hospitals, and poison-control centers should be posted near the phone, along with parents' numbers.
- Does each child have a "cubbie" or place for private belongings?
- Are the space and materials adequate for the number of children served? Can a child have privacy and quiet when he or she wants to be alone?

Parent Involvement
- Do parents and staff share basic values of interest to you? What are staff opinions on encouraging cooperation, or discouraging

racial and sexual stereotypes? What kinds of books and pictures will be influencing your child?

- Are there any difficulties with allowing you to stay with your child a short while during the first few days if you are able to and want to?

Program Activities

- What goes on in a center or day-care home on a daily basis? Is there a routine so children know what to expect? Is there a variety of play and learning activities available?

Family Day-Care Contract

If you have located and chosen a family day-care provider you feel comfortable with, you may be asked to sign a contract with your provider. This can make all expectations clear and avoid any one of a number of misunderstandings which could get you and the staff off on the wrong foot. If your provider isn't currently offering contract agreements, you might consider asking him or her to sign a contract if you feel it would be a good idea.

The following sample is one suggested by the Child Care Resource Center and could be modified in any ways you feel are appropriate to your own situation.

Sample Contract

The following is an agreement between (*parent*) and *provider* concerning the care of _____, (birth date), and _____, (birth date).

Hours and Fees:
Child care will be provided between the hours of _____ and _____, at a fee of _____ per hour or per week. The parent also pays an additional _____ per ½ hour when late in picking up the child at the end of the day. The parent agrees to make an effort to contact the provider by _____ on days when the child will not be coming. The fee includes _____ but not _____, which the

parent provides. Provision for payment for sick days or vacation days: _____

Other conditions:
1. The parent gives consent for the provider to take the child for medical care in an emergency.
2. The child may ride in a car with the provider as long as a seat belt or approved infant-care restraint is used.
3. The parent will notify the provider if anyone else will be picking the child up from day care. The following people are authorized to do so: _____.
4. Both parent and provider will give each other ample warnings (___ weeks) about vacations, termination of services or other changes.
5. The parent will not bring the child to the family day-care home with a contagious illness, fever or (*other*).
6. The parent will leave a complete change of clothing, appropriate for the weather, at the family day-care home.

This agreement is effective from _____, 19__ until _____, 19__. Fees may be renegotiated on _____.

Parent's signature _____ Date _____

Provider's signature _____ Date _____

Your Responsibilities
Child-care providers, by and large, are not paid exceptionally well for the very important services they perform. Once you find a good worker you can show your appreciation by viewing her as a professional and not abusing her services.

- Make sure her schedule is understood and that you are on time when bringing and picking up your child. Find out now if there is an extra fee for lateness.
- If you are occasionally unable to pick up your child on time, give your provider a list of any friends or relatives who are authorized to do so.

- What about vacations and holidays? Sick days? Ask how much notice you should give if altering your schedule.

FINANCIAL ASSISTANCE FOR CHILD CARE

If you are a person of not too many means, how do you afford child care? More than half my paycheck would be gone before I ever saw it.

If you are currently working at a well-paid job, or have support payments to supplement your income, you may have no problems paying for child care. Otherwise, you may be able to find a program that can help you out with financial assistance.

Federally funded programs are quite limited (for example, the Head Start Program), but your state may have money available for other programs. As an example, those now being offered to disadvantaged parents in Massachusetts include: Department of Social Services (DSS)-Contracted Day Care (formerly called Title XX); Title IV-A (Income Disregard); Voucher Day-Care Project. Check with your local social-services office to see if similar programs are available in your state.

DSS-Contracted Day Care. To receive Department of Social Services funds in Massachusetts you do not have to be on welfare, but you do have to meet two requirements regarding service and income needs.

(1) Your gross income cannot exceed these levels:

For a family of:	*Your maximum income must be equal to or less than:*
2	$12,216
3	15,096
4	17,964
5	20,844
6	23,712

(2) You must also have one of the following "service needs": You (a) are working at least thirty hours a week; (b) are re-

ceiving job training or undergraduate college study; (c) are in a Work and Training Program (WTP); (d) have a mental or physical incapacity; (e) have a child with a verifiable disability—physical, emotional or intellectual.

DSS-Contracted Day Care applies to only programs that have DSS contracts. Funds are allocated on a sliding scale; parents pay a portion based on income level and DSS pays the remainder. Often there are waiting lists.

Title IV-A (Income Disregard). To qualify for Title IV-A funding, a woman must currently be receiving AFDC and must have begun work. The first thirty dollars earned each month and up to one-third of the remainder does not count against her welfare payments. Day-care service is paid for by the family and then reimbursements are made through adjustments in AFDC grants.

Vouchers. If you are eligible you may receive child-care information and referral from your local Voucher Management Agency (contact your Department of Social Services), and vouchers to partially cover day-care cost. Providers must be licensed. To be eligible you must (1) be receiving AFDC, (2) be recently out of work, or (3) be working or in a training program approved by the Work and Training Program.

Head Start Program. Head Start is a federally funded program which provides free preschool programs for children aged three to five. If you are receiving AFDC, SSI, or General Assistance you are automatically eligible. You may also be eligible if your child has a disability or because your income falls below these levels:

Family Size	Maximum Income
2	$6,220
3	7,760
4	9,300

(over 4 add $1,540 for each person)

Private Funding. Check to see if the centers you are interested in have raised funds either to provide scholarships or to offer a sliding-scale fee to those with low or moderate incomes. If you are interested in a cooperative day-care plan, you may be able to reduce the cost somewhat by putting in a certain number of hours each week or month.

Also check with your employer to see whether your company sponsors a child-care center in the community or at the work site, or whether your company provides its own voucher system to working parents.

You should, in any case, inquire about whether your firm's benefits package includes child-care support in any way. If enough parents ask, it is much more likely employers will begin to take some responsibility for the current lack of private-industry aid. If you find yourself working with a number of other single mothers, you might get together to plan a proposal for your employer (who could take advantage of tax breaks now being offered for setting up a local center) to which mothers could contribute.

Tax Credits
Don't forget to check on your entitlement to a tax credit on your income tax (currently between 20 percent and 30 percent) for child-care expenses. Contact your local Internal Revenue Service office or income-tax preparation service to find out exactly how much credit you are eligible to receive.

References

Belle, Deborah. "Social Ties and Social Support," *Lives in Stress: Women and Depression,* ed. D. Belle. Beverly Hills, Calif: Sage, 1982.

Bequaert, Lucia. *Single Women: Alone and Together.* Boston: Beacon Press, 1976.

Child Care Resource Center. Pamphlets. Available from 24 Thorndike Street, Cambridge, Mass.

Curtis, Jean. *A Guide for Working Mothers.* New York: Simon & Schuster, 1975.

CHAPTER TEN

What If I Need Welfare?

With all the trouble, mismanagement, unjust decisions, and in-competence ... I think welfare still helps women keep their fami-lies together and keep on going.

As a single mother, your chances of needing welfare someday are much greater than if you were a man with child-support re-sponsibilities. Divorce or death of a husband often brings a sudden dramatic shift in life circumstances. And for some mothers welfare becomes a way of holding the family together. It may come as a surprise to discover that one out of every three single mothers applies for welfare (but only one out of every nine single fathers).

In case you should need welfare someday, it is helpful to know what this emergency support system can provide for families. While welfare can help smooth your path should the going get rough, it also has pitfalls. Unless you are prepared for them, your experience is likely to be less productive than it could be. And it may be more traumatic than necessary. Wel-fare, a confusing system, needs to be put into economic perspective before we take a look at what it can mean for you, and what it means for other women who become—short-term or long-term—"welfare mothers."

WELFARE IS A WOMEN'S ISSUE

As confusing as the welfare system can be, one thing is clear: Welfare is a women's issue. Why is this so? There are three main reasons, all related to money:

- Because the average woman still earns less money (increasingly so) than the average man—57 cents for every dollar a man earns. Women are concentrated in relatively few occupations, more than half of which pay poverty-level wages.[1]

- Because women still provide the bulk of children's economic support in single-parent homes. Ninety-three percent of all women are awarded custody of their children in divorce cases, and most of these women cannot count on child-support payments from their ex-husbands. Unfortunately, fathers are still not generally held responsible for ongoing child support once they are no longer in the home—either by the legal system or by society in general.

- Because there are too few government- or private-industry-supported child-care facilities. And, by and large, there are no alternative options to the nine to five workday, such as flextime or split-shift schedules.

Women are living longer today; they get divorced much more often; and recently more unmarried young women are having babies. For these reasons the percentage of families headed by women rose from 10.1 percent in 1950 to 14 percent in 1976, an increase of about 40 percent.[2]

But while more women are becoming single heads of households, the ability of women to support their families is declining. The average woman earns less, in relation to the average man, than she did twenty years ago. This is despite the greater number of women in the work force, an increasing number of women in higher-paid professions, and affirmative-action programs. As Diana Pearce points out in her article in *Working Women and Families,* women—unlike immigrant groups who worked their way up from the bottom of the labor market—have stayed on the bottom. Pearce notes that other things being equal (age, race, education, and residence), women who head families would receive 36 percent more income if they were men.

So what does this mean? That given women's present earning potential and child-care responsibilities, millions of women are finding it impossible to make enough money to support their families. When no other options exist, many women resort to government aid, primarily Aid to Families with Dependent Children (AFDC).

THE GREAT ESCAPE?

> It doesn't make sense to me . . . the way they set it up and then blame women for not getting out of a trap.
>
> —BONNIE NATHAN

The AFDC system doesn't make sense to Bonnie Nathan, or to many other women who participate in it. The system doesn't even make sense to a lot of "intake" workers who see the system from the other side of the desk. AFDC is full of contradictions. It has a high personnel-burnout rate. And it has a high dissatisfaction rate among those it serves. AFDC payments in most states are already below the poverty level. But AFDC and other programs available through welfare departments inevitably appear the most likely candidates for cutbacks whenever there is talk of reducing the federal budget.

AFDC has become synonomous with "welfare"—although it is only one of the programs offered by the government. AFDC provides ongoing financial assistance for children whose parents are unable to support their families on their own. Assistance is given in the form of periodic checks, with which a mother is supposed to pay rent, utilities, and other basic living expenses. These payments (see the sample budget later in this chapter) vary enormously from state to state, but generally provide a family with an income that is below the poverty line.

In addition to AFDC checks, a parent may also—if eligible—receive supplements from other programs (primarily food stamps, medical coverage (Medicaid), and work-training classes). There is no simple and general formula for determining what any mother is eligible to receive. Benefits in San Francisco or St. Louis would not be the same. Budgets are based primarily on family size, amount of total income—including child-support payments—and personal assets. But it takes, as one supervisor at an AFDC office said, the proverbial Philadelphia lawyer to calculate exactly what an individual family may receive. Further complications arise because rules are continually being changed.

If you have just separated from your spouse and have no income, or are now struggling along on a part-time income, a trip to your local AFDC office can provide you with the information you need about a monthly budget and supplemental programs you may be entitled to. It is, however, recommended that you read this chapter thoroughly and, if possible, see a welfare-rights advocate before you apply for AFDC.

As far as much of middle America is concerned, welfare provides the Great Escape from work for millions of people they view as "welfare idlers." Most Americans are unfamiliar with how welfare actually operates, and for whom. They believe their tax dollars are supporting individuals who could and should be in the work force. Stereotypes of the "welfare cheat" survive, even though in 1974 national surveys of welfare fraud by the U.S. Commission on Civil Rights found only 3 percent of all cases showed eligibility errors—and these were primarily the results of agency mistakes.[3]

Others, however, see welfare as a massive, national trap for women, an agency that provides mere bread-and-water income to those who have no access to well-paying jobs. An even stronger criticism of welfare has been made by some individuals who feel welfare helps continue the cycle of women's poverty—mainly by providing a continual pool of cheap labor for big business. They maintain that welfare offers no incentives to move up and out, and that it can, in some cases, wreak havoc with a woman's sense of pride and dignity.

Does the welfare system provide any kinds of solutions for women in poverty? How does it operate? And does it reduce or contribute to mental-health problems for women and their children? These were a few of the many questions the Stress and Families Project asked when it interviewed women who have had experience with the welfare department.

WHO ARE "WELFARE MOTHERS"?

The stereotype of the woman on welfare is that she has too many children, is young to middle-aged, often black and undereducated, and doesn't want to work. But women receiving AFDC cannot be so easily lumped into categories. Overall, they run the gamut from very young to older women, from very healthy to extremely ill, with about the same number of children as other women nationally.

- In 1977 the U.S. Department of Health, Education and Welfare (now the Department of Health and Human Services) found that 64 percent of all AFDC families have only one or two children.

- Women come from a wide variety of economic backgrounds—from upper- and middle-income families, and from blue-collar or poverty-level families.

- Most women use welfare as a temporary way station. Less than 10 percent of those who go on welfare become heavily dependent on the system (that is, receive 50 percent or more of their family income this way for nine or ten years).[4]

- Most women have worked and expect to work in the future. At least 90 percent of mothers in AFDC households have been employed, according to HHS. The women interviewed by Stress and Families had extensive work histories, many beginning work at a very early age, and expected to work in the future.

total stranger. It makes you feel like a fool to tell how you've been deserted and are completely helpless. Even so, they wouldn't give me money until I had taken out a warrant against my husband. That's what you have to do if your husband has deserted you. Even after that I had to wait until my application was processed and a check mailed. That was about three weeks.

When women apply for welfare, feeling helpless and at the mercy of those who are in charge, a sympathetic intake worker or caseworker can make the experience less painful. But many workers fail to provide support and encouragement. Some are actually hostile.

Worker Burnout

While a third of the women interviewed said that their caseworkers were competent and dependable, 60 percent said that they experienced negative treatment—indifferent, rude, or even hostile. As one woman said, her caseworker acted as though she were "taking the money out of her own pocket." Some women were harassed by other workers connected with the welfare system. This happened to Bonnie Nathan.

No one was rude to me at the welfare office when I first applied. But when I went to take out a warrant against my husband I was intimidated in the worst way by the woman I had to talk to.

She was very insulting. Very heartless. She was an older woman who had become hardened, having been in that particular line of work for so long. She was not at all sympathetic that I had been abused by my husband. The first thing she asked me was how could I have gotten involved with a man who was so irresponsible. I tried to explain that you never know what kind of situation is going to develop in a relationship with another human being.

But she just kept throwing out those kinds of remarks, just to be mean. I was in a very hurting position at that time and I wasn't in any state to be pounded upon by someone so callous. And I just broke down. She had me in such a state I couldn't reply as I should have to defend myself.

It appears that due to the nature of the job, even the most well-meaning and generous-spirited man or woman can eventually turn into a machine, and a nasty-running one at that. This may be less of a problem in better-managed offices, or where the case load is realistic for the workers. But many offices are understaffed and overworked. The combination can mean that frustrations are passed down the line to AFDC applicants.

Make It Easy on Yourself: Your Checklist

The following suggestions may speed up the process of application for welfare and make it as painless as possible for you.

Realize that application is not likely to be a pleasant task, but if you know what to expect things may go more smoothly. Whatever the cause of your application, you are probably feeling needy and a little out of control. So try to buffer yourself as much as you can. If possible, don't wait to go until you are down to your last nickel, or until a week before the baby is due. Pick a day when you are feeling relatively calm and decisive, and expect to spend several hours to complete the process.

Find out as much as you can before you go. Call ahead to be sure you apply at the proper office and ask when the best and least hectic times of the day are. State offices vary in their overall programs, but here are some of the things you may encounter regardless of what state you are applying with:

Guidelines for eligibility. Generally, AFDC benefits are available in the case of absence, death, incapacity, or unemployment of a parent, but the guidelines are complicated and constantly changing. So it is difficult to determine without a visit whether you are eligible or not. If your husband is deceased you will need:

- A copy of the death certificate;
- Proof of any Social Security benefits you are eligible for.

If you are legally separated or divorced or your ex has deserted the family, you will need to provide:

- Legal proof (a divorce decree or separation statement) *or*
- You will probably have to sign a Self Declaration of your spouse's "continued absence" (currently defined as twenty days away from home).

Documentation. In addition to the above-mentioned documents, you will probably need to bring:

- Birth certificates for your children, showing their ages and their relation to you;
- Proof of residence;
- Personal identification, i.e., Social Security card, driver's license;
- If you are working, your last three paycheck stubs;
- Title to any car you own and indication of any money still owed on it.
- Checking- or savings-account books. (To demonstrate eligibility, you are permitted no more than a minimum amount of personal cash and property. Check with a welfare-rights advocate to determine the current amount you may be permitted.)

Have your facts and figures together and attempt as much as possible to look at this as a business transaction, which it is. The more you can speed up the work of the department by being businesslike, the faster your application should be processed (but don't count on it). Having necessary information with you can also save you an extra trip to bring the missing documentation.

Be prepared to be asked about the events that led to your application. If you have been married and your husband deserted the family you may have to swear out a warrant against him. This will entail another set of procedures, such as going to a different office to process additional forms.

Be prepared for minimal amounts of sympathy, but don't be hostile. Most intake workers and caseworkers are only trying to do their jobs, under very frustrating circumstances. Even the nicest intake worker has heard a similar story hundreds of times before and may be feeling a little burned out or helpless at being unable to do more.

Whenever possible, talk to other women who have applied for AFDC or have, in some way or other, information about the system. If possible, ask a knowledgeable person to go with you when you apply. An informed friend or welfare advocate will buffer some of the discomfort of application and may increase worker responsiveness. If you don't know anyone who has previously applied, try a women's center or an information hotline, the newspapers, or your phone book to see if any welfare-rights advocacy groups are listed near you.

Because of state variations, it is difficult to provide information that is applicable in all locations. Someone in your immediate area should be familiar with local rules and regulations.

Do ask specifically about the following possibilities if the information is not volunteered:

Medicaid. You should automatically be eligible if you are eligible for AFDC. You may be issued a temporary card while your application is being processed and if you have immediate health-care needs. Medicaid can feel like a safety net. It can save you a great deal of money on treatment for yourself and your children. Be sure to ask what Medicaid does not cover. Among items women have reported as unavailable to them under Medicaid are orthopedic shoes with braces, intrauterine devices, some vitamins, certain cold preparations, and some prescriptions. (Not all doctors will treat Medicaid-insured patients. To avoid hassles, if you are seeking a new doctor be sure to ask, before you go for a visit, if he or she accepts Medicaid payments.)

Food stamps. You may or may not be eligible, depending on your level of income. If you are unemployed, these should definitely be part of your benefits package.

Work and Training Program. If you have children over six years of age, you may automatically be requested to sign up for a work program. From all accounts, this program is not functioning especially well at the moment; sometimes it proves useful, often it doesn't. Some women report that the training offered to them was only for very low-paying jobs. Talk to a welfare-rights advocate about how you might best profit from involvement, or how to avoid this requirement if you feel overqualified for what is being offered.

Rent subsidy possibilities.

Educational benefits (*Basic Educational Opportunity Grants*). These may include tuition or transportation supplements. If you are now in school or interested in returning to school for additional education, the department of social services may prove helpful.

Confusion

Even for women who have been receiving AFDC for a while, learning the system is difficult because information is fragmented. As one woman said, "It's a hassle each time! Welfare has a book of rules and regulations (the Welfare Manual) but it's impossible to get the information and the updates. They don't want you to have it so that you never know your rights and what you can get."

Confusion may result, in part, from the numerous changes that are continually being made within the welfare department. (Food stamp regulations, for instance, may change every few months.) But some workers may be reluctant to provide women with all the information they have. One woman applied for AFDC after a fire had destroyed most of what she owned. When she called the welfare office on her own, the man there was reluctant to speak with her, let alone provide the information she needed. But when a welfare advocate went with her the man's attitude changed dramatically. She said that without a welfare advocate she would never have known what she was entitled to receive.

A welfare intake supervisor, however, tells another story. From a worker's point of view, bureaucracy is the culprit. Eligibility standards are complicated, and once the last complicated rule is learned it is soon replaced by a new one. The following examples illustrate the workers' dilemma. Once a woman was automatically excluded from participation in a work training program if she had a child under six years of age.

Now exclusion depends on whether she works more than thirty hours a week or leaves her child for a "continued absence" of more or less than fifteen hours. Families used to be eligible for AFDC until a child was eighteen or still in a secondary school or other advanced educational program. Now families are no longer eligible for AFDC if children are over eighteen and in college, but *are* eligible if children are over eighteen and in a vocational program. These are just two of the innumerable confusing stipulations.

Delays

My landlord was really getting to the point, like what's going on? My rent was getting further and further behind and he was really getting on edge. I explained to him that I'd applied for welfare, even showed him the letter once I got it, but it was taking so long.

Even after application with a responsible and efficient intake worker, do not expect to receive benefits immediately. Women reported delays of two weeks to two months.

Word from the welfare department is that automation has considerably speeded up the application process recently and promises to reduce caseworkers' loads. Local offices are now required to complete all procedures within thirty days. Complications, however, may arise if offices do not have all the information they need. So it will be to your bennefit to make sure you have supplied all information accurately. This should include whether or not you have ever received benefits from another office in any other location.

Lack of Privacy

What I've found to be the worst thing is that you have no privacy. If I should call up right now and say something bad about my neighbor to her social worker, what I say would be believed. They'll go and check on her, or him, and give them the third degree. Anyone who wants to call up and tell a lie is believed.

When you become a welfare recipient, you own nothing, not even privacy anymore. Everything that you ever had in your life belongs to the welfare department. This includes your bank account, insurance, anything that you might want to leave to your children in case something happens to you.

Lack of privacy is an aspect of welfare that many women find very demoralizing. In exchange for government aid, women open up their lives like pages in a book. Because of the regulations of AFDC regarding minimum allowance for personal property, the system takes on monitoring functions. In some areas, investigators have dropped in to check on personal property. Many women feel welfare has infringed on their personal rights and dignity.

The less sure women are of themselves at the time of application, the more likely they are to feel mistreated. This is why it is essential to find out about your rights before application. You do have certain rights to privacy and there are some questions you simply don't have to answer. A local welfare advocate can give you the specifics you need.

HOW MUCH CAN I EXPECT FROM AFDC?

Welfare benefits vary substantially from state to state. In Texas, AFDC payments are extremely low. In New York State they are relatively high. But regardless of where you are now living, on welfare you will not be living in luxury. It is likely that with a lot of budgeting and perhaps a part-time job, you will still barely be making ends meet.

Nationally, 94 percent of AFDC families headed by women are living below the poverty line. The following scale is that currently in use for determining budgets for families in Massachusetts. It may give you some idea of what to expect.

For a family of:	2	$314.20 per month
	3	374.20
	4	444.50
	5	509.70
	6	575.10

It is apparent that only the hardiest can survive on welfare, so be sure to ask about any other benefits you may be entitled to, such as food stamps or Medicaid, that can help you stretch your dollars. Even so, it will be tough. Here is what one woman said about living on her current budget.

"Now I get five hundred a month. That sounds like a dynamite amount but a hundred and seventy automatically goes out for my rent. And another seventy automatically goes out for heating oil. That is two hundred and forty immediately. They used to say you shouldn't pay more than a third of your income for rent, but this was the cheapest apartment I could find. I'm paying half my income on rent.

"Over here there is no public telephone anywhere around, so I have to have a phone. And electricity. And for some stupid reason you might have to eat. Or the kids' shoes wear out. Welfare doesn't think of that. They don't allow for the extras. Sometimes it comes down to do I buy shoes or do I buy food? I don't know where those stories come from about the welfare mother who buys furs and takes cabs. It's cut right down to the bone."

For most women, continually coping with money shortages on welfare takes a toll on their mental and physical health. It is doubly difficult for those who feel guilty about being on welfare but find the system offers no help to get up and out. In fact, some welfare practices can actually encourage women to stay dependent on the system, as limited as it is.

MAKING IT

There is no denying that welfare can be of invaluable assistance to the single mother who finds herself in crisis. But it is obvious that welfare does not provide a positive lifelong alternative to becoming financially independent. Women who remain on welfare for long periods are more apt to allow the negative features of welfare to dominate their lives. Awareness of limited options and lack of control in their lives proves unhealthy. Depression can result. And long-term depression can create its own set of difficulties, making it even more difficult to move up and off welfare.

Those women who have been most successful in using the system have:

- Viewed welfare as a *temporary* safety net;
- Made it a point to find out all they could about what is available. (Some have been able to use welfare training programs or educational opportunities to create stepping-stones to better paying jobs. A young child doesn't have to be a handicap to doing this. One woman who took her baby to college classes with her said that she felt this actually gave her an edge—her professors felt she was more mature than other students!);
- Actively fought against the depression that can result from coping with day-to-day difficulties of limited budgets and feelings of lack of control;
- Kept active and kept their goals in sight (for more information on goal setting see Chapter 3);
- Periodically arranged some time away from their children;
- Continued to improve their self-images (as described in chapters elsewhere in this book);
- Expanded their networks of other women and men who could give them the information and encouragement they needed to help them move forward.

Source Notes
1. Diana Pearce, "Women, Work and Welfare: The Feminization of Poverty," *Working Women and Families,* ed. K. W. Feinstein (Beverly Hills, Calif.: Sage, 1979).
2. Ibid.
3. Nancy Marshall, "The Public Welfare System: Regulation and Dehumanization," *Lives in Stress: Women and Depression,* ed. D. Belle (Beverly Hills, Calif.: Sage, 1982). Unless otherwise indicated, data for the early part of this chapter is based on the work of Stress and Families Project staff member Nancy Marshall, Ed.D., Harvard University.
4. M. Rein and L. Rainwater, "Patterns of Welfare Use," *Social Service Review,* 52 (1978), 511–534.

CHAPTER ELEVEN

Sex and Love in Your New Life

As a single parent, you are coping not only with the eternal and universal concerns about sex and love but with problems not encountered by married women or single women without children.

- When to introduce a lover to your children—and when not to?
- What to do if your children want a new Daddy so badly that they try to marry you off to the mailman, the Little League coach, and the pediatrician?
- How to deal with your child's inevitable jealousies and hostilities toward a new male acquaintance?
- What to say when your son marches into the living room and tells your male friend it's time he went home?
- What to do when your daughter starts flirting with your lover?

These questions are unique to the single mother. You may be answering them easily and naturally, to your own and your child's satisfaction. Or you may be feeling you need to rethink some old habits and values to deal with these new questions in the best way.

This can be an exciting but scary process. And it can be

especially difficult when you are aware that what you are doing feels right for you but it is not what you would choose for your child. For example, today many single mothers have sex with, or live with, their lovers without marriage. Yet a number of women say they would prefer their daughters to wait until marriage before having sex.

As a single parent you will probably experience days when you worry about how best to get your personal life together without creating conflicts for your child. The advice of "experts" is often contradictory. In the end, many women fall back on their own intuition, or talk their questions over with other single mothers who are in the same love boat.

It can be tough making decisions on your own, but remember that solo parenting offers you unique learning and teaching opportunities. You no longer have to deal with the opposing values that often arise in a two-parent household. And because your personal options are more open-ended now, it is possible to help your child develop less restrictive attitudes as well. As Jane Adams, author of *Sex and the Single Parent,* says: "The opportunities we have to mold the sexual attitudes of our children are actually greater than those available to nuclear families, because what is normal in most two-parent homes is rather narrow, but what is realistically normal in human sexuality is very wide."

You may be well aware of the part your parents' attitudes and actions played in your own sexual development. And you may sometimes fear that mistakes of the past will permanently alter your own child's development. But remembering that you are only one influence in your child's life may help lessen your fear of making the wrong move each minute of the day. A child's ultimate approach to love and sex will result from his or her own particular personality and from a variety of encounters with the world over many years. Some of these influences are discussed in this chapter.

Mothers are, however, the most influential sources of information during a child's formative years. So your attitudes and the level of your honesty can set your child sailing toward adulthood with some sense of confidence—or with apprehension. To help your child steer a course as fearlessly as possible, ask yourself how closely your words match your feelings and actions. If you think that your child can't tell when you are being fully honest, you are underestimating his or her perception.

It will become easier to match your behavior with your verbal advice to your child as you grow more comfortable with yourself as a loving, sexual human being. This process is one of continuous unfolding. It is not automatically completed when we come of age. Expressing ourselves honestly can be difficult, especially when our own inheritances have been somewhat repressed or lopsided.

This chapter will explore some of the ways that you as a woman may have received less than your full legacy of love from your family and larger society, and what you can do about it. We will also explore particular concerns for single parents today. As you read on, ask yourself which inheritances have played the greatest part in shaping your attitudes. Then you might ask whether you are passing on similar or altered legacies to your child.

VARIETY IS THE SPICE

According to Adams, five out of six divorced parents reestablish sexual relations within one year after marital separation. This may mean infrequent, casual contact, a monogamous full-time relationship, or a variety of experiences in between. Obviously, sex plays an important part in single mothers' lives. But how important varies from woman to woman.

Some women find that singleness offers them an exciting range of new intimate possibilities. Many women with limited premarital experiences are surprised to find they are capable of much more heightened sexual encounters than those they shared with their ex-husbands.

There are women who explore sex with a number of different men and others who find intimate involvement difficult to establish. Opportunities for meeting new men and attitudes about sexual involvement vary widely. Children's needs (imagined and real), and one's levels of self-esteem and self-confidence also play major parts in determining how sexually active a woman chooses to become.

Some single mothers are very comfortable with their own sexuality and find themselves facing few barriers to resuming their sex lives. But for many women, especially those who never fully dealt with sexual inhibitions in their marriages, singleness brings the need to reexamine personal beliefs and values.

YOUR SEXUAL VIEWPOINT

How would you answer the following questions?

	TRUE	FALSE
1. Sex was never a taboo topic in my parents' home.	____	____
2. I grew up with the idea that intercourse would be a pleasurable experience.	____	____
3. My first sexual encounter was enjoyable and made me feel good about being female.	____	____
4. I enjoyed intercourse with my ex-husband and felt it was a mutual exchange (I got as much as I gave).	____	____
5. I am satisfied with my current/last intimate relationship and find/found it fulfilling.	____	____

If you have answered "true" to these questions, your sexual legacy has been rich and rewarding, one that too few women receive from their families, lovers, and larger communities. If you have answered "false" to a few or more questions, now may be the time to explore your personal inheritance of sexual attitudes and myths. How have they affected your view of yourself as a woman and your interactions with the men in your life? And how do they affect what you are passing on to your children?

Learning to See Our Sexuality

How do we learn to see ourselves as women? Of the main ingredients that go into the sexual recipe, one is the impressions, spoken and unspoken, that we pick up from our parents and other family members (too often translated as "good girls don't . . ."). The second is the combined influence of friends and peers. The third comes from interactions with the larger world: from literature, television, and other media, from teachers, traffic cops, and other members of our extended society. A fourth, and very important ingredient, is the nature of our early sexual experiences—how skillfully and lovingly (or ineptly) we are given firsthand information. How do these factors work?

Research shows that from the first day of life the way infants are treated depends on their sex. Girls learn very early that they are like Mommy in more ways than they are like Daddy. And how does Mommy feel about sex?

Nonverbal clues play an enormous role in communication. If your mother enjoyed touching your father, and welcomed his evening hug at the door, your mother didn't have to tell you she enjoyed intimacy and actively appreciated sex.

If her shoulders tightened when her husband reached out to touch her, you may have gotten the distinct impression—no matter what she actually said out loud—that intimacy was probably not a very pleasant thing. Later, if she told you that sex was something you would just have to "put up with" from your husband someday, your worst fears would have been confirmed. All such positive or negative attitudes set the stage for the character you imagined you would play in bed. What did your mother tell you without words? And what did she tell you about sex directly?

The Larger World: Friends and Enemies

Some people tend to lay all blame for their sexual problems at their mother's feet. Various branches of psychology encourage them to do so. But this is as unfair as it would be to insist that the nutritional habits of an adult are totally determined by the meals he received at the age of ten. Genetic factors and one's total environment help shape the individual also. And the environment outside the home is something no mother has control over.

Once a child grows through his preschool years, he is ready for his first major step into the outside world. Up until this point a mother may be able to channel most of the information a child receives. Mother can choose his books and often his playmates. With a lot of effort, she can decide which movies and television programs are most appropriate. And she can decide which would be too frightening, violent, sexually confusing, or simply inappropriate.

Money, of course, has an enormous amount of influence on the kind of environment she can create at home. Life in a housing project will provide a more intrusive set of variables to cope with than life in a private home with a spacious backyard, safe within a wealthy community.

But once a child begins school, each mother must deal with the fact that her child will be influenced by many others, individuals she may not know at all: school officials and teachers, a variety of play and schoolmates, perhaps religious instructors, cafeteria workers, bus drivers, and street-crossing guards. Each of these individuals—to a greater or lesser degree—will influence your child's sense of the world and who he or she is in the world.

From others your child will learn how to share possessions, knowledge, and emotions. And she will also pick up feedback on her own sexuality through sexist or nonsexist textbooks, graffiti in rest rooms, children's informal sex-information networks, remarks of teachers and individuals on the street, and later probably through a formal class in sex education. Indirectly, your child even receives part of her sexual legacy from the past.

How the Past Plays a Part

Although you and your child have been born into the twentieth century, you are still partially shaped by the recent past. Some influences have been helpful to women. Others may create conflicts for you as you reevaluate your life as a single parent.

Each culture has always defined adult love and sexual mores in its own way. In addition, within each society men and women are assigned different sexual roles. Some of these differences have served to repress women's sexual feelings. Female children in some African societies, for example, still experience the removal of their clitorises, and some have their vaginas sewn shut to ensure their virginity before marriage. (These and other practices are discussed in Andrea Dworkin's book, *Woman Hating.*) But the psychological conditioning practiced in the Victorian Age served the same purpose for many of our mother's mothers.

In old attic trunks or in velvet albums we can find aging photographs of our grandmothers and great-grandmothers. They or their mothers arrived here—as immigrants, indentured servants, or slaves—from a hundred countries, but there is often a common look in their eyes. Our white grandmothers and great-grandmothers were not called slaves, as their black sisters were; but their bodies were still not really their own. Usually they stare at the camera grimly, unsmiling. Their backs seem straight as pokers. They were stiffly encased in yards of cotton or muslin or silk, their skirts falling completely to the ground. Maybe the tips of their laced shoes peek out, but that is all, because it was considered suggestive to expose their ankles.

We know that underneath their long dresses they were yet further separated from their bodies by layers of slips and pantalets and whalebone corsets. Dozens of buttons locked them into their dresses, all the way to their necks.

We can't be surprised that these women who stare back at us

often look so grim. They were products of the Victorian Age, when women were not supposed to have sexual feelings. They were told that only those who were sick or somehow perverted—"ladies of the night"—ever felt pleasure in their own bodies.

Millions of women were so overwhelmed by the repressive attitudes of their society that they believed in the myth of woman as nonsexual creature. They remained virgins until they married, and then they lay in bed at night staring at the ceiling thinking of God or country or children while their husbands "took their pleasure." Whether men had sex in silence, with slight or intense embarrassment, or simply with grunts and groans, that was men's business.

Our grandmothers' lack of access to their bodies was paralleled by restrictions in other areas of life. Few of them traveled freely outside the home, entered into the decision-making areas of trade and business, owned property, or offered opinions about anything but children. Women forced to work had more physical freedom, but they faced starvation and dangers of life on the streets, for they were usually poorly paid domestic or factory workers or street vendors.

Sex and Science

Are we really out of the dark ages in our attitudes toward sexuality, or are we still working through myths of our own psychology and sexuality? What has science offered to replace repression?

	TRUE	FALSE
1. Women are born with a sexual capacity as great as, if not greater than, men's.	____	____
2. In some societies, frigidity is an unknown condition.	____	____
3. Sexual arousal that never ends in orgasm can lead to chronic lower back pain, headaches, and other physical and mental illness in women.	____	____
4. Left to her own devices, a woman can usually reach orgasm within a few minutes.	____	____

5. Fifteen minutes is not an unusually long time for
   a woman to reach orgasm during intercourse.   ____   ____
6. Almost half of all men ejaculate within a few
   minutes after penetration; many within seconds.   ____   ____

The answers to all of these questions are true.

Science obviously has its place in the exploration of human behavior. But the misconceptions of some "experts" have caused
continuing damage to generations of men and women. For example, while Freud's theories broke through many of the Victorian preconceptions about women, some of his ideas simply
created new myths.

Daringly for his day, Freud suggested that women do indeed
have sexual feelings. But he maintained that women were basically inferior copies of men, biologically and psychologically.
And because of what he interpreted as women's "penis envy,"
he painted a picture of woman continually searching for a
penis substitute, never reaching her full potential until she had
created a substitute object in the form of a male child.

Not until women entered the field of psychology was the logical assumption made that it is not men's penises women envy,
but their power.

Until recently, so few women were prominent in the physical sciences, sociology, anthropology, and other fields that
the "experts" on the nature of female sexuality were all men.
Some male investigators were simply misguided; others so
blatantly misread women that it is hard not to believe their
"discoveries" were born out of their own personal conditioning. Though some helpful knowledge emerged, views of
women's sexuality have contradicted each other and spread
other confusions.

Once told by doctors that we were incapable of any sexual
enjoyment, now we are told that we are all potentially insatiable sexual machines. We get the distinct impression that all
"real women" have multiple orgasms at the drop of a hat.

Pushed slowly to adopt men's views of what sex is all about, some women are beginning to suffer the same performance anxieties that men do. What an irony that where once women felt compelled to lie and say they felt nothing, now many women lie and say they are overcome with passion! Women have been driven to a twentieth-century phenomenon: the Fake Orgasm, possibly more familiar to many women than the common cold.

Personal Experience: The Final Ingredient

If your attitude about sex is tied up with a long history of negative words and associations, it will not be surprising if sex is not, as one woman said, "number one on my hit parade." Were you warned against masturbation, did you hear sexist comments often, lack open discussion time for sexual topics, start your first period in secrecy, glean information as a child from neighborhood black-market books? Often lack of information leads girls to fashion the most fantastic ideas about how one gets pregnant. ("I thought if I sat on a man's lap I could expect a kid in nine months.")

If misinformation is not corrected by counterknowledge or with positive experiences with men, there may be great difficulty in establishing normal and enjoyable sexual relationships. Unfortunately, many young girls are subjected to encounters that only reinforce their negative impressions of sexuality—encounters that may vary from one mildly abusive event to years of trauma, such as frequent rape by a brother, father, or other relative. (Louise Armstrong's recent book, *Kiss Daddy Goodnight,* is an excellent, easily readable treatment of how incest can affect girls' images of themselves and their sexuality.)

For many women the first experience of intercourse is positive and their lovers help to counter early negative conditioning. For others, first intercourse simply confirms their anxieties and fears. This is especially true if their lovers are as inexperienced or as misguided as they are. Too often men come to sex with their own mythologies and are so busy trying to carry them out that they fail to contribute to a positive and loving mutual experience. If a man is too busy worrying about how long he'll be able to maintain an erection, or has been primed with the thought that only he is supposed to enjoy sex, the turnoff for a woman may be complete.

FINDING PERSONAL MEANING

Obviously, putting the pieces of the sexual puzzle together can be very confusing even for an adult. For a child, the issues can be baffling.

While you cannot control the welter of conflicting and confusing information your child may pick up from her environment—she wouldn't develop confidence and her own sense of self if you did—you can help her.

If you make attempts to keep communication channels open, you are assuring your child that you will be there to help her make sense of what she finds in the outside world. Your child will be more likely to keep you as a reference source if you:

- Establish yourself as home base. Ask your child to come to you first with any questions she may have. Let her know that if you don't have the answer, you will help her find it. But don't pry if you sense your child is not ready to share her thoughts with you. Constantly asking what is on her mind may only make her more reluctant to confide in you. And reading diaries and private notes is a no-no. Children need privacy too.

- Attempt to provide honest information and understanding, not judgments and punishments. One woman said that as a seven-year-old she went to her mother to ask about a confusing word she had seen written on the bathroom wall in her school. Instead of a definition of the word she received a slap across the face from her mother, and was told never to repeat the word again.

- Prepare for sex-related questions and for the repetition of sexual slang your children may pick up from playmates. Whether you like it or not, children are exposed to the world at an earlier age today, and it is likely your child will also begin physical maturation at an earlier age. If you don't have the answers to questions that she is liable to ask, or if you are unfamiliar with sexual terms, check with your friends or your librarian, and be prepared.

Showing embarrassment or anger will only give your child the idea that sex is a taboo subject. If, due to your own past conditioning, you are simply unable to discuss sex openly with your child, buy or recommend a book appropriate for her age group. You might want to give it as a gift, along with a note or short talk that lets her know it is not the subject itself, or her curiosity, that is making you uncomfortable, but the way in which *you* were taught about sex.

- Show love and respect for others you care about in platonic ways, as well as with physical gestures. Then your child is more apt to integrate sex and love into her behavior toward others when she reaches adulthood. If you have a son, you have a unique opportunity to allow him more space for emotional and physical expression than his father may have been permitted in his day. Hugging is one good place to start. Boys who have never been permitted to cry, to hug, to say I love you, often end up as men who have no idea how to begin affectionate lovemaking.

- Respect your body, and your child's body. Healthy individuals are aware that their bodies are gifts. Encouraging your child in sports, dancing, gymnastics, bike riding, or in any number of activities the two of you might like to share, will help her become comfortable with her body. And teaching her to care for her body as she would a fine instrument is a lesson that can be taught early on.

- At some point, preferably before your child reaches puberty, explain to her that sex is a natural instinct, and that people have always used their bodies to express love and experience pleasure. Sex is not just for producing babies. This may be difficult for you if this concept conflicts with your religious beliefs. But your child needs to know that the sex drive is often independent of love, and that it is a part of the body's natural processes.

Too many young girls grow up believing that if a boy wants to have sex it means he feels undying love. The rising number of pregnant teenagers may indicate that some vital information is lacking somewhere.

- Make sure your child understands that just because you may want to keep your sex life private, it doesn't mean that sex is something you are ashamed of. You may want to explain that expressions of love through sexuality are like your innermost thoughts; you don't share them with your neighbors but keep them for yourself.

THE "AVERAGE" WOMAN

The sexual capacity and potential of women is at least as great as men's and exceeds their capacity in some areas. But for the reasons previously discussed, the average woman probably:

- Fits somewhere in between a total lack of interest in sex and group sex with whirlpools and whipped cream;
- Has had pleasurable moments of sex, but fewer than she's capable of;
- Knows how to reach orgasm within a few minutes if she puts her mind and hand to it, but doesn't, according to Masters and Johnson, experience orgasm as consistently during intercourse;
- Is not as communicative as she might be about expressing her own preferences during foreplay and intercourse (and the men she usually sleeps with may not oblige with sensitivity and skill even if she did say clearly what she wanted);
- Finds enjoyment in areas of sexuality that many men don't dwell on, like affectionate gestures, words of love, and unhurried kisses on her neck;
- Has faked an orgasm or two (or many) in her lifetime and still isn't quite sure whether to be a "total woman" she should feel pleasure mainly in her clitoris or in her vagina, or both.

GETTING THE MOST OUT OF SEX

On some days women may feel so aroused they could spend hours in bed with a sensitive lover; on other days, sex is the last thing they have on their minds. Men have always permitted themselves this range of sexual interest. For three straight weeks they may be workaholics and hardly remember they have a penis, and then suddenly they want to make love on the kitchen table because of how good their wives' buttocks look bending over the sink.

Strangely, men don't consider this inconsistent—in themselves. But women are supposed to have one attitude and one only—a continual state of receptivity, "ready-but-not-too-ready." As with everything else but mothering, women have been assigned a passive role. Many men are actually unnerved at a woman's responsiveness in bed, and are totally confounded if their lovers suggest more than ten seconds of foreplay before insertion.

If you are not getting or sharing what you want, you may find it necessary to educate your lover from time to time. This may feel awkward at first, but you, after all, are the real expert about your own body and what you may want to do with it. What should you keep in mind?

Positive sexual interactions include at least six ingredients that our grandmothers and many of our mothers were not always able to bring to their lovemaking. These are:

- Making sure you connect with the kind of man *you* are interested in having in your home and in your bed. This is a learning process for many single mothers. If you have limited experience, making a list of what you are looking for, and what you simply don't want to deal with, is a good place to start. Later in this chapter we'll discuss where to connect. But it is essential to know what qualities you are looking for in potential lovers.

- Being comfortable with your body, knowing what you like and what you don't like, what makes you feel good and what—regardless of the advice in sex-technique manuals—just doesn't interest you.

- Being able to communicate clearly. For the maximum mutual enjoyment, you may need or want to take an active role in expressing your preferences and dislikes. Feeling free to set limits is as important as being willing to explore. This can be especially difficult if you have been taught that men always lead, or if the current man in your life feels he is always supposed to know best. Some women have found that assertiveness-training courses have been helpful in teaching them personally acceptable ways to make their needs known.

- Setting realistic goals for the relationship. Good sex doesn't usually happen overnight (in fact, most first encounters are much less satisfying than the passionate, perfect portrayals in romantic novels). If you are naturally shy, and your lover has a history of premature ejaculation, it's highly unlikely that you are going to see stars for three hours the first time you get together.

- Making sure the timing is good for you as well as for your partner. Feeling pressured into sex is a sure way to create an experience you will end up resenting. Not allowing enough time, or bringing to bed worries over the children, will also put a damper on sex and make it less enjoyable than it could be.
- Taking adequate birth control measures is a must. If you are worrying somewhere in the back of your mind about getting pregnant again, your ability to "be there" in the moment will be severely hampered. Depending on your religious beliefs, you may not be totally comfortable with the idea of birth control, even if an unplanned pregnancy could severely disrupt your life. Only you can make the final decision, after weighing your priorities. But talking to other women in your situation may prove very helpful.

WHAT CAN WE EXPECT OF MEN?

Does your lover:

- Provide you with limited and/or unimaginative foreplay?
- Often conclude intercourse prematurely, long before you are satisfied?
- Display a general lack of tenderness and gentleness in lovemaking?
- Withdraw too quickly, and roll over and go to sleep?

These are some of the complaints often made about the failures of men in lovemaking. Sometimes women take these actions personally, feeling they indicate a lack of love on the part of their partners. But often these are simply indicators of the limited experiences of sharing and expression that men bring to sexuality.

To express sensitive and intimate emotions and actions as an adult, it is helpful to have learned such behavior early in life.

But boys, to a greater extent than girls, are taught to limit their range of expression. Boys may grow up feeling comfortable with their bodies, but they are often cut off from expression of deep emotions. ("Big boys don't cry!" And "big boys" quickly learn that kisses, hugs, and words of love spell "sissy.")

For men who have been taught not to show emotions, or who haven't learned how to help others express theirs, sex can come to mean a brief grappling in bed before ejaculation. Sex may be equated with the act of penetration, compartmentalized into that half hour of unimaginative, unemotional intercourse on Saturday night.

Other men know that something more is expected of them, but they are afraid to admit they aren't quite sure what that something is. A smaller percentage of men have gone far beyond macho; they are not embarrassed to be honest about what they don't know, or to express what they do. They are willing to explore, and are aware that the mind cannot be separated from the body in creating a satisfying experience. No matter how good a technique, without emotion, sex is as mechanical as a well-executed game of Pac-Man.

Sex in the broader sense is the way people interact with each other in any loving way. You are expressing your sexuality when you hug a friend, or when you hold hands walking down the street. Limiting sex to hurried intercourse is like limiting meals to fast-food hamburgers.

Men who are willing *can* learn to modify their ideas about sexuality, although some men, like women with long histories of negative conditioning, may need professional help. Most men are willing to try to modify their behavior if they believe it will enhance their relationships.

Women who freely express their needs and preferences give such men concrete information to which they can respond. Men also feel that some of the pressure for performance lifts a little when they are not working in the dark, so to speak. How can you help modify and enhance sexual behavior?

- Good sex begins with caring honesty. You can't expect your lover to read your mind. Although it may feel risky at first, or simply awkward, get into the habit of truthful communication, in and out of bed.

- Let your lover know when he is pleasing you—and ask him to let you know when you are doing something he especially enjoys. Communication after the fact is less valuable than in the present. Saying later, "Well, if only you had. . . ," can cause feelings of inadequacy over a past attempt to please you.

- Phrasing should be encouraging and instructive. We all like to hear feedback about what we are doing well; it makes us much more receptive to hearing constructive criticism. For instance, you are more likely to achieve positive results by saying, "That doesn't feel as good as when you. . . ," than by starting out with "You are doing that all wrong!"

  As you become more adept at active expression and find yourself occasionally taking the lead, it is likely that your lover will feel freer to express a wider range of his emotions. That is the glowing possibility of positive mutual exchange: Doors are opened into rooms within both you and your lover, doors you may never have felt permitted to open before.

- Relax! Sometimes sex is just plain fun.

WHAT DOES BEING A WOMAN MEAN TO YOU NOW?

> I don't feel feminine the way I used to. I mean I'd like to sit here and take an hour and experiment with makeup, dress up in heels, and the whole bit. But I don't have time. I rush to my morning classes and then to my afternoon job and then home to the kids. When I get home I put on one of these goodies—my sacks I call them, comfortable but not exactly Ms. Alluring.

Some days it may be all too easy to forget that you are a woman as well as a single mother. Often the idea of "femininity" is lost among the roles of mother and father, of nurturer, worker, and disciplinarian. Playing two roles sometimes means that any concept of what it means to be feminine is drastically changed. But while you may be viewing yourself as less and less sexual (and feeling that way because of all you have to balance), others may view your altered status very differently.

DO MEN TREAT YOU DIFFERENTLY NOW THAT YOU'RE A SINGLE WOMAN?

It used to be when I was married I'd visit my friends and be very comfortable with their husbands, have a cup of tea or whatever. After I was separated, women started treating me differently, and some men did too.

The irony of your present situation may be that while you are viewing yourself as less feminine, others may have a much more heightened awareness of you as a woman. Some women are surprised and hurt to discover that they are viewed as threats by their married friends, and as "fair game" by some husbands or old male friends. These subtle or not so subtle changes of attitude can be unsettling.

After a divorce or separation, you may, upon occasion, be made uncomfortable by the altered interest of a friend's husband. You may even be faced with a proposition when the husband of a friend "drops by" unexpectedly.

You are not responsible for the advances men may make, but it is wise to take some precautions to keep yourself out of potentially hurtful situations. Even if you later explain to a friend that her husband got a little out of line, it is likely that your friendship just won't be the same.

ASSESSING YOUR CURRENT NEEDS

What you may be looking for in a man right now might not in any way resemble what your neighbor or your best friend has in mind. Since only you know what kind of a man is going to satisfy your current needs, take a few minutes to think about and set some priorities. Taught to be the subordinate one in a relationship, you are all too likely to find yourself in a compromise situation unless you are clear about what you want.

Some single mothers find that what is missing most from their lives is someone to help share the load and laughter. They aren't looking for Mr. Sex; they'd be happy with a nice guy who would respond to a request to pick his socks up off the floor. Maybe you'd like, as one woman put it, "another body round the house, someone who's good company but would give me some space."

Other women who have felt confined and bored by their marriages would just like to have "a good time for a while; nothing serious, just someone to go out with on weekends . . . maybe go dancing or out to dinner now and then." Some women feel they just aren't ready for another heavy involvement. Others would prefer to be remarried tomorrow.

Defining what is important to you will help keep you out of uncomfortable situations, and prevents wasting your time. If, for example, you hate crowds and are not into music at all, you're liable to have serious conflicts with a salesman who lives to party and dances until dawn. If you are a confirmed animal lover, you can be sure you will have difficulty relating to a clinical scientist whose life work is based on experimenting on dogs and cats. Whatever your needs are, be honest about them from the beginning and you probably won't get too far off track.

Some women will never feel really happy until they are remarried; others become addicted to the freedom they find as single women. As one woman put it: "Jimmy can be a dominating person, but Jimmy does not own me. I never realized before that a woman needs some kind of freedom, at least I do—and not just when a man thinks of it. It just wouldn't occur to me to say, 'Hey, can I go to the Y tonight?' The way I feel that would never happen to me now. But once I was like that."

Some women always seem to be attracted to the underdog. Not knowing their own strengths, they may shoot too low and wind up not expecting enough from men. This is one reason a good support network is invaluable to you as a single woman. Friends provide each other with positive feedback and sometimes just the right amount of objectivity that is needed. If you find yourself blinded by a flashing smile and big brown eyes, your friends are there to remind you that your standards may be slipping, even though the chemistry feels just right.

How much time do you want to invest in a relationship right now, and what are your communication needs? Maybe you'd be happy with a quiet, unobtrusive man who is content to listen rather than to speak, one with whom you can share long, comfortable silences. Maybe what turns you on is a nonstop talker, the man who must talk life through in order to understand it, and expects you to be right there joining in.

Knowing what you need can save you a lot of time in the long run, and will give you a better idea of where and where not to look. If you'd enjoy a four-hour conversation about the life-style of the Trobriand Islanders, you might get it with a graduate student or a sociologist. But most likely you won't find it with an off-duty bus driver or an accountant.

MEETING MEN

If you have only recently become a single woman again, you may be a little out of practice at scouting out your local territory. The last decade or so has brought so many changes that now women are free to go and do most anything they like—things undreamed of in the last generation. You have a choice of many more places and ways to meet men than ever before; most of them are considered "respectable" by all but the most conservative. But you may have to be a little more active than might be immediately comfortable for you. Especially in larger city environments, men expect a little help with connecting, and passivity is considered a bit passé.

It may take a little while to regain the knack of being open with strangers. But there is no time like the present for exploring.

If it has been years since you went out with anyone but your ex, you might consider the "practice date"—an evening with a male friend, or a man who may be more interested in you than you are in him. If you feel the stakes aren't so high and you are not in a make-or-break situation with Mr. Wonderful, it can make the dating transition a little easier.

Remember that men are everywhere, not just clustered in singles bars. It is often not so much where you are, but your level of openness that will determine whether you connect with someone or not. It is just as possible to meet someone interesting in a bookstore, walking your dog, or at a yard sale as at a party. So be prepared for the possibility of an encounter at all times.

Once you start getting out and circulating again, make sure that you are going places that are fun or interesting. And go with a friend whose company you enjoy. That way if you don't meet any interesting men you won't consider it a wasted evening. If you are out solely to find a lifetime partner, it is bound to show.

Where to Go

- To avoid the Saturday Night Singles Club Seizures, try getting a babysitter one late afternoon or early evening every few weeks or so and explore the "Happy Hour Haunts" near your place of work. This has many advantages over weekend jaunts: Drinks are usually less expensive (often two-for-one) and it will give you a chance to relax after work now and then instead of rushing home to your second job. Often free hors d'oeuvres are served, so you can munch out and keep your alcohol intake balanced. And you may find the atmosphere a lot more relaxed than on weekend date nights.

- Sports events. Check out basketball, football, baseball games, or hockey matches. Spectator sports events are usually filled bleacher to bleacher with men and you never know whom you might end up sitting next to. Try skating, skiing, bowling, or other participant sports that attract men. If you are not athletic, you may find darts, overwhelmingly male dominated, at local night spots.

- Local adult courses or college classes. Courses are now being offered to adults in everything from accounting to yoga. Taking a course in something that interests you may lead to meeting men who share your interests.

- Woods and wilderness groups. If you are an outdoors type, you may find it worthwhile to join an organization like the Sierra Club or a local hiking club that sponsors jaunts and trips. One of the most interesting is the organization of American Youth Hostels (AYH). There is no age limit to membership and a nominal annual fee (around ten dollars) entitles you to very inexpensive overnight facilities at any of about three hundred sites in the United States, and numerous sites in many other countries. Many AYH sites accommodate children as well.

- Causes. One of the most satisfying ways to meet others with similar interests is to contribute some time to a favorite cause. This may be especially helpful if you have been battling depression for a while. The quickest cure is action; it can benefit you and those around you. Do you have an interest in any of the following?

Animals. Check your phone book for a local Audubon Society; Greenpeace (if you are interested in saving the whales); the American Wildlife Federation (which takes action on the world front as well as at home); or a local animal shelter, Humane Society, Animal Rescue League, or protection service.

Theater or music. Your interest in the arts could lead you to volunteer at a community theater, begin a drama group, help with a drive to renovate or create an arts center, or join with others to attract musical groups to your area.

Self-help economic groups. Your despair over inflation could lead you to find or help start a food coop, a consumer information center, or a child-care resource center for working parents.

History. Historic interests could lead to contacts at a local museum or historical society.

Politics. Political frustration can turn into political action through volunteer campaign work for a promising candidate. Or you may want to join a group working on political reforms in your area.

Social Causes. The hurt and anger of one woman who lost her daughter because of a drunken driver has recently led to the reform of drunk-driving laws in several states. The coalition of concerned parents which she helped form has proved remarkably powerful and effective.

Your social concern can also be channeled into raising funds to combat rare diseases, into establishing homes for battered women or children, or into some other cause that moves you personally. The point is, you can increase your sense of power and control and at the same time possibly meet just the kind of man you are interested in. But it takes some action on your part. An added side benefit of work with social causes is that it may remind you there are others in the world with more immediate problems.

- Parenting groups. While they are fewer than women, single male parents are often looking for the same kinds of solutions to parenting problems as you are. These groups often sponsor social activities—dances or dinners where parents can mix socially—as well as meetings where common problems are sorted out.

- Blind dates. Most every woman has a blind-date story, about the interminable evening at the amusement park with a midget who had bad breath, or of fighting her way out of Jack the Ripper's speeding car. But many women do connect with interesting men through friend-arranged dates. Nothing is ever guaranteed, and your friend's taste is probably not exactly your own. But at least friends do have your best interest at heart and can usually be counted on for some amount of discretion. A good policy to pursue may be to try anything at least once.

- Classifieds. If you are not interested in computer-dating hookups (which are becoming more numerous and sophisticated all the time) but are shy about face-to-face encounters, you might consider the growing number of classified possibilities. Most major papers and some magazines are now carrying personal classified ads for singles who are tired of the usual dating approaches. Some indicate primary interest in sex, but many individuals are truly looking for more well-rounded relationships. Classifieds allow you to indicate exactly what you are looking for, and to do preliminary screening (replies are sent to postal boxes and kept confidential).

SEX AS BARTER

Sooner or later as a single woman you may be tempted by someone to use sex as a bartering tool. Since men are often apt to place more emphasis on your sexuality now that you are a single woman, you may find yourself propositioned in the oddest places and for reasons that have nothing to do with affection.

Without a full-time man around some man sometime will likely offer you a service in exchange for sex. It may happen with your landlord if you are having trouble paying the rent some month; it may happen with your mechanic when your transmission goes; even with your doctor or your boss.

How you handle a situation like this depends on a number of factors, including, of course, how you feel about the man involved. If your mechanic is a sexy single man you've been intrigued by anyway and you are stuck in a snowdrift, you will probably consider his offer. If he is a macho-minded Quasimodo, the choice may be an easy no. Again, only you have the right to determine the appropriate response. But it is good to keep in mind that any relationship that is not entered into freely will probably make you feel like a victim on some level. Without feeling control and willingness, you may wonder later if the barter was worth it.

OVERNIGHT GUESTS

> As a mother, I just can't be as free as I'd like to be. When men want to stay over I'm very aware of how that might affect my kids.

Undoubtedly, children complicate your sexual life as a single woman. Some men are apprehensive about getting involved with a woman with children. Others view mothers as inherently desirable and are anxious to meet and get to know their children, often long before mothers feel comfortable with extending the relationship in that direction. How your children feel is another matter.

Young children may simply be interested in having a Daddy around again and may try to couple you up with every man you meet. Children closer to or into their teens may be very threatened by the men you meet and date. They may even resent the idea of having another man in the house.

Some women become so guilt-ridden and intimidated by their children's opinions (fearing that admission of the need for companionship and sex will be somehow damaging) that they either close off their own needs, or hide them. This solution is unlikely to benefit either you or your children in the long run. If you don't let your children know that you are a woman with a need for adult companionship, as well as their mother, you are presenting a false front to your family.

Establishing your own needs clearly and firmly without defense may be the best approach to the question of dating. But be sure to pay close attention to verbal or behavioral changes in your child that indicate s/he may be upset with a new man in your life. When children are feeling insecure, they may revert to earlier behavior patterns: tantrums, withdrawal, bed-wetting, thumb-sucking, or anger may indicate their fears of losing you, or their resentment at spending less time with you.

Understanding your child's fear, and allowing expression of that fear before you attempt to give reassurance, can help. But be prepared to find that one quick assurance of your continued love will probably not be enough for a child who seriously fears a strange adult may take his place, or may replace his father. This fear may be especially strong if your child unexpectedly finds an overnight guest in your bed in the morning.

Some women find it easiest to reserve overnight dates for those weekends when the kids are with their ex-husbands. Other women feel that if they like a man enough to sleep with him there is no reason not to have their children meet him in the morning. Many adopt compromise solutions, such as having a lover leave before morning, especially if they are not seriously involved. While sorting out your own decisions about dating, here are some things to keep in mind.

- Most children are likely to be threatened to some degree by the men in your life. Exceptions to this are children who are feeling very much in need of a substitute father.

  If you want to avoid getting your child's hopes up over a man you are not viewing as a prospective partner, it may be best to avoid at-home bedroom situations which your child may associate with his father.

- Misconceptions about sex can increase a child's anxiety. Because sex can look violent to a child, a chance sight of Mother in bed can appear as if "Mommy is being hurt." It is a logical assumption for a young child to make, and if this situation occurs you may compound the confusion if, in embarrassment, you order your child out of the room and never explain how deceiving appearances can be. Some reassuring explanation is in order to allay your child's fears. To prevent such a situation, consider getting a lock for your door.

- Many mothers are aware that children often believe they are the cause of their parents' divorce. So they try their best to explain why separation occurs, often talking at length with their children, with or without the aid of one of the numerous children's books explaining divorce. But women sometimes forget that their child may be experiencing the same kinds of guilt and hurt feelings over the loss of a man they have come to view as a friend or a substitute father. Should your child lash out at you after your breakup with a lover, he may be needing reassurance that he is not to blame in what may appear to be a recurrent theme of attachment and loss. Whether or not your child shows any signs of disturbance, it is best to let him know that it is not his fault your relationship did not work out as you'd hoped.

BIRTH CONTROL AND SOCIAL DISEASES

As a married woman, an unexpected pregnancy may have complicated your life but not totally confounded it. As a single mother, an unexpected pregnancy may set you back years.

Now that you are the main support for yourself and your family, it is vital that you understand the pros and cons of the birth-control options now available to women and men.

Recently separated women are often embarrassed to ask their doctors about birth control. The same is true about fears of venereal disease. Women may fear censure and disapproval—and indeed, some doctors seem all too ready to include preaching with medical practice. If you feel uncomfortable discussing these issues with your doctor, either take a firm stand on your own body rights, or change doctors.

Unless you insist that every man you sleep with use a condom, it is quite possible that sooner or later you are going to find yourself with a vaginal infection. Infections don't necessarily mean herpes or gonorrhea; simple diseases like Monilia or Trichomonas are more common. Unfortunately, venereal disease appears to be an increasing possibility with sexual encounters; some doctors feel it is reaching epidemic proportions. Possibly this is because more women are taking responsibility for birth control, so fewer men are using condoms—the one fairly secure method of preventing vaginal infections. Put simply, the more men you sleep with, the more your chances of becoming infected. Knowing how to get prompt diagnosis and treatment is essential, since even milder diseases can have serious consequences if left untreated.

Signs of infection are often masked, so periodic gynecological checkups are very important. An immediate appointment is called for if you suspect an infection. (See *Our Bodies, Ourselves* by the Boston Women's Health Book Collective for a thorough discussion of venereal diseases.)

References

Adams, Jane. *Sex and the Single Parent.* New York: Coward, McCann & Geoghegan, 1978.

Armstrong, Louise. *Kiss Daddy Goodnight.* New York: Harcourt Brace Jovanovich, 1979.

Boston Women's Health Book Collective. *Our Bodies, Ourselves.* New York: Simon & Schuster, 1979.

Dworkin, Andrea. *Woman Hating: A Radical Look at Sexuality.* New York: Dutton, 1976.

Masters, William, and Virginia Johnson. *Human Sexuality.* New York: Little Brown, 1982.

Seaman, Barbara. *Free and Female.* Fawcett Publications, Connecticut, 1972.

CHAPTER TWELVE

Working Women: From Roses to Rivets

It is always a risk, trying for a job. Sometimes you'll win. Sometimes you'll lose. But you aren't going to lose every time!

Chances are, if you are a single mother you are familiar with one or more of the following hassles relating to the world of work:

- You have an uneasy feeling that you still don't know where you could or should be going at this point in your career. You can't *quite* imagine the next step from here.
- You feel your résumé is lopsided, with low-paid, service-concentrated jobs intermittently broken up with time-outs and/or detours.
- Your job allows you to pay the bills—just barely. There is rarely anything left over at the end of the month for a savings account or investment.
- You know that there is a much better job for you "out there," but you aren't plugged into an energetic information network that could tell you just where that job is.

These are just a few of the problems you may be facing now if you are among the majority of working women. About 80 percent of the 43 million women now in the paid work force are currently employed in the "white-collar ghetto" or blue-collar "support industries."

And there are a few other things you may be discovering at this point in your career. Although legislation is supposed to have outlawed employment discrimination and regulated equal access to educational and training programs, most of the women you know and work with are still:

- Earning only 56 percent of the average man's annual income;
- Receiving no assistance from the government or from private companies to help with their child-care needs;
- Not among the mere 5 percent of women holding managerial positions or among the 4 percent of women in higher-paid craft and trade positions.[1]

WOMEN, WORK AND WAR: THE LAST FORTY YEARS

World War II dramatically altered the state of women and economics. As men were drafted, millions of women, almost overnight, were forming the labor backbone of America.

When veterans returned from that war, they were rewarded by medals of valor, medical disability when needed—and their old jobs. But for women, it was, in a way, a step backward—to kitchens and nurseries and poorly paid jobs. And it was a step backward into myths of women's inability to handle responsibility.

While almost forty years have now passed since Rosie the Riveter and Maggie the Manager were everyone's neighbors, the seeds planted at that time have begun to bear fruit. If some women were content to forget that they had ever played vital and well-paid roles in the economy, other women were not. A women's movement arose, strong enough to create legal changes in the social and economic structure of the United

States. Agencies were set up to prevent further segregation of women workers and to make the wealth of the country more accessible to those women who wanted and needed to work for their share.

But although legislation has been enacted, enforcement is a slow process. Especially slow have been the changes in attitude that must occur before employers willingly and enthusiastically open doors to the male-dominated, higher-paid occupations. Some women are making it in the world of work—particularly in medicine and law. But not all women have yet achieved their goals. And only a small percentage of single mothers have reached the more satisfying rungs of their chosen job ladders.

This chapter provides information that will enable you to shoot for jobs that will give you the salary and personal satisfaction you seek. No one formula will work for all women, because women are now scattered among a thousand different occupations at all levels of work experience. This chapter offers advice for women who are "Starting Out," for those "Moving Up," and for those who want "A View from the Top" and are willing to compete with men for those very limited slots.

Wherever you are now on this continuum, you can make your work life more successful. One way is to become aware of some of the common barriers to success you are most likely to encounter. Seeing the barriers clearly will enable you to go through them, or around them, to get where you want to go.

Perhaps—without being a charter member of NOW or chief speaker at your trade union meetings—you have already come face to face with some of the barriers that keep millions of women all around the country from getting ahead.

BARRIERS TO SUCCESS

Lotte Bailyn, of the Sloan School of Management at the Massachusetts Institute of Technology, has examined three main kinds of barriers to achievement in women's professional lives.

The Professional World. What is actually available to a woman "out there" is, says Bailyn, the first consideration. But the levels and types of discrimination a woman is likely to encounter are also important. Whether a woman finds at least one role model can be crucial. Imagine that flying a plane is an appealing idea, for instance, and that you have the natural skills to pursue aviation as a career. Since only about 2 percent of all pilots are women, you will have little opportunity to meet a woman pilot who could reinforce your desires and encourage you to pursue your goal. In fact, it might not even occur to you to try for a career in aviation if you've never seen another woman attempting to do so. Outside circumstances such as these are frequently powerful deterrents to women seeking to expand their horizons.

Adult family life. Another factor that Bailyn sees as a potential barrier is a woman's "adult family life." Many studies have demonstrated that support—or lack of it—from the men in their lives can influence women's success. The occupations of those men are also important. Many men are threatened if a woman moves ahead of them in status or in salary. Because such men find it very difficult to encourage women to succeed, women feel forced to choose between moving up in a job or threatening the egos of their lovers.

The number and ages of their children can also affect how fast women will be able to get into the work force and how long they will stay there, as well as the amount of time they can devote each day to getting ahead.

Your personal perspective. In addition to market influences and family life, there are barriers to achievement that each woman carries around with her. Even the most successful woman may still carry seeds of negativity which are the result of the early care and training she received from her parents and teachers, of her birth order (whether she was the first child, who received strong pushes toward achievement, or the sixth child, who received a very different level of encouragement and attention), and of other unique factors such as natural talents and inclinations.

* * *

For purposes of convenience, the forces that can slow down or speed up a woman's growth in her job life have been divided into "internal" barriers—those which women can overcome only by rearranging their own perceptions of themselves—and "external" barriers—those erected by institutions and other individuals that all women have to deal with.

In whatever field you have chosen—or will choose—work will be a positive and rewarding experience only when you have learned to deal with these barriers. Some are common to all workers—men and women; some are unique to working women.

INTERNAL BARRIERS

Wishful Thinking: The Trap of the Kept Woman

"Kept women," whose main jobs may be decorating million-dollar houses and providing support and martinis for their husbands at 7 P.M., still exist but are becoming an endangered species. Although being kept may sound like fun, nonworking women are today such a minority that you are not likely to become one of them.

Even if you were to "luck out" and meet a man who could afford to support you, there is little security in dependency, as millions of "displaced homemakers" have found out. The increasing rate of divorce and shorter life-spans for men mean that a woman must become responsible for her own lifetime security. Only if you are "a going concern" will you be financially secure. Only if you continue to make yourself marketable will you really be free from the anxieties of worrying about tomorrow.

While most men have always had to face this rather unpleasant reality, many women still cling to the illusion that their working life is going to be a temporary situation. Yet the average married woman is now spending twenty-five or more years in the workplace, the average single woman around forty years. When work is viewed as temporary, it is never given adequate attention. This may be the hardest reality of all, but eventually—if you want to hitch yourself to a work wagon that will take you places you want to go—you will have to:

- Stop viewing work as a temporary inconvenience until Mr. Money comes along;
- Start thinking of your work life as a career—not as a series of unrelated jobs.

Fear of Success

How often have achieving women been called "pushy" and "aggressive"? How often have we heard the term "castrating bitch" applied to a woman who believes her own goals are as important as those of the men around her? Seldom is a man at the top considered unsuccessful. But a woman at the top is often assumed to have lost her "feminine nature" along the way. This is a fear that many working women can relate to. If you fear that success—in almost anything but motherhood—may divorce you from men, or create jealousies among your friends, you will have second thoughts about doing everything possible to climb up the work ladder.

Matina Horner, president of Radcliffe College, has identified this fear in women and labeled it Motive to Avoid Success. This fear can create such conflict in a woman that she denies her own abilities. On the job, it can lead to self-defeat. Rather than risk being labeled "unfeminine," many women will forgo the pleasure of putting their talents to fullest use.

This phenomenon has been observed in girls not yet out of high school—excellent scholars in their younger years, they suddenly stop working for high grades because their popularity is threatened with their boyfriends and peers. They fear being called "goody-goodies," "snobs," or "brains," and it takes a strong will to continue achievement in the face of these put-downs. No one wants to be the oddball, at any price; and few teenagers want to face the possibility of dateless nights.

Many women opt out by choosing early motherhood. This provides a perfect excuse to discontinue competition and can be a temporary reassurance of femininity. But this appears not to be a successful escape, as Horner points out: "Unfulfilled abilities, interests, and intellectual potential give rise to feelings of frustration, hostility, aggression, bitterness, and confusion. . . ."[2]

Have you ever purposely played into your own fears of success? Have you ever chosen to appear less competent than you knew you were? Most women at one time or another have asked the "big, strong man" to open a jar (a relatively harmless personal put-down). But have you ever bitten your tongue rather than correct some piece of misinformation a man passed on in conversation? Or were you completely understanding and accepting when a man in the office—with less ability than you—was promoted into that job you should have had? Almost every woman can think of times when, to prove her womanhood, she has been less than herself.

In personal relationships this kind of put-down can serve to damage self-esteem; in the workplace the fear of appearing competent can keep you in a dead-end job for years. This fear can be lessened by:

- Remembering that competent doesn't mean being a "pushy broad," except to a very threatened man, and it doesn't make you "masculine." All persons have a right, and in fact an obligation to themselves, to be as whole as they can become. If we pretend long enough that we "simply don't understand mathematics" or "have no idea what all those little metal things are" under the car hood, we are effectively blocking our own growth and sooner or later it's likely we'll be sorry we did.
- Remembering that children are always watching you, and the more competence you display the more opportunity they will have to observe effective behavior and expand their own talents. Marjorie Lozoff, of the Wright Institute at Berkeley, points out in "Fathers and Autonomy" that "children who perceive their mothers as inadequate come to associate femininity with indecision and immaturity."[3]

Risk Taking

Connected inextricably with wishful thinking and fear of success is barrier three, the little voice that so often says "I'm going to fail if I try this, so why bother" or "I'm not really qualified/capable/don't have as much of whatever it takes." This little voice, born of insecurity, can keep you from applying for a better school or a better job, from doing active future planning, and from seeing yourself in a position of greater responsibility. It is pervasive.

This voice is inside the heads of most of us at some point or other. It is a fear of appearing stupid, of revealing weaknesses, of taking risks.

Sometimes the fear of risk taking can be dealt with by reason:

- Make a list of all your skills and accomplishments, and reason with your fears by reminding yourself how often you have managed, supremely well, in the past; or

- Get some reassurance from good friends (or a therapist if your self-esteem has hit rock bottom). Friends help us move on because they can often see our good points better than we can. Without friends and other supportive people in our lives, the little voice (usually based on negative experiences or conditioning from the past) may be the only one we are able to hear.

At other times there is no way to deal with the voice except to blot it out and leap. To succeed at whatever you choose to do, you will simply have to learn to take risks from time to time; that is how you get places. It may be helpful to play out a scene in your mind, to think of the worst thing that could happen if you apply for that manager's position or suggest to your boss that you would be the best woman to go to next month's conference. As one woman said, "Sometimes you'll win, sometimes you'll lose. But you aren't going to lose every time!"

EXTERNAL BARRIERS

Availability

While there are more than twenty thousand different jobs in the United States today, most of those jobs are not available in your backyard, or even in your city. If you have your heart set on learning to grow fruit trees and starting your own orchard, Manhattan is not the place to begin.

Unless you are willing to relocate for the job of your dreams, you have to take a realistic look at the market and what is available within commuting distance.

Discrimination

Thus, in the United States, discrimination against women combined with a high incidence of marital instability have helped to increase the incidence of poverty. We have estimated that about two-thirds of the poverty among black and/or female-headed families with working heads is due to discrimination.

—BARBARA BERGMANN
Department of Economics,
University of Maryland

As much as people would like to believe that discrimination has ceased to exist just because it has been outlawed, prejudice is alive and thriving in the workplace. Because it is such an unpleasant idea, many women are unable to acknowledge it has an effect on their lives. Though the exact number of women affected is unknown, it is apparent that sexual bias is a potent force in holding women down. You may be fortunate enough to have had a good run of job experiences which didn't involve any overt discrimination. But sooner or later it will most likely be a factor you will have to deal with.

Groups like the Ku Klux Klan are so blatant no one can ignore their existence. Sexual discrimination is often harder to pinpoint. It may have surfaced in your ex-husband's expectation that even if you were working you were supposed to be doing all the housework as well. It may have occurred to you when a man on the street made a lewd comment as you went by. In the workplace bias occurs in a male's unspoken assumption that "his" secretary will pour coffee and take care of his personal correspondence or pick up his laundry. And it is very apparent in the pay differentials between men and women who do comparable work.

On the personal level, discrimination is a daily force in lowering women's self-esteem; this is especially deadly because it directly affects our sense of who we are and what we think we can accomplish.

Black women tend to be more aware of discrimination because they face it as blacks as well as women. Often white women can temporarily maintain the illusion that it is something that happens to others. Unless you learn to recognize it and to deal with it, you will be shortchanged sooner or later.

Discrimination occurs in all fields and on all income levels. Whether a woman is a professor or a clerical worker, her paycheck is lower than that of a man doing comparable work. In fact, women with college degrees earn significantly less than men with fewer years of education, as the following figures from "9 to 5," the women's office workers organization, demonstrate.

Occupation	Median Year of School Attained	Median Earnings (est.) 1970	Median Earnings (est.) 1985
MALE INTENSIVE JOBS			
Truck Driver	9.0	$9,660	$16,160
Auto Mechanic	10.5	9,070	13,270
Deliveryman	11.7	9,060	12,720
FEMALE-INTENSIVE JOBS			
Retail Salesclerk	12.7	6,470	9,480
Bookkeeper	13.7	6,540	9,600
Typist	13.7	6,070	8,890
Secretary	13.9	6,860	10,100
Registered Nurse	14.2	8,090	11,970

Discrimination is not going to go away overnight, because it serves a purpose for the discriminator: It can be used to keep women's wages low or to keep women "in their place." Only through women's increasing awareness of unequal treatment, and their *action* to eliminate it, is this negative force weakened.

Fighting Sexism One to One Though no simple answers exist for discouraging sexism you encounter from individuals, there are some guidelines. Often men (and women) are unaware that they are prejudiced because prejudice has become a lifetime habit. The form of discrimination called sexism is so prevalent *you* may not always be aware of it when it occurs on a daily basis. But women learning to get ahead simply can't afford to be seen in a stereotyped way, as Margaret Higginson and Thomas Quick point out in *The Ambitious Woman's Guide to a Successful Career.* They offer some suggestions that can help.

Don't sanction sexism anywhere you find it—whether in an office joke that puts women down or in references to women's anatomy. When you hear remarks you find discriminatory, consider the following:

- Avoid the immediate charge of discrimination, since this is likely to put a man (or woman) on the defensive.

- Ask for an explanation of the remark; pretend not to understand and ask for a rationale for the comment.

- Be direct, but not hostile or bitter. This is easier to do if you don't take the remark personally (if it wasn't meant that way) but view it as a general put-down of all women. "Would you say that to a man?" and "Why do I have the feeling you said that because I'm a woman?" are two examples offered by Higginson and Quick.

- Focus on sexism as the issue, not on the person who is showing bias.

- Don't allow comments to build up; deal with them as they come along so you don't end up with a backlog of anger.

- Whenever you can, show support for men or women who are trying to overcome their sexist conditioning.

Fighting Institutional Sexism If you believe that you have been discriminated against in hiring, firing, or promotion practices, contact groups that can give you specific advice as to how to handle the problem:

- A local women's center, if there is one near you
- A feminist lawyer
- The local chapter of the National Organization for Women
- Your trade or professional union (if you are employed)
- If all else fails and you are prepared for a time-consuming case, get your facts together and send them to the Equal Employment Opportunity Commission, which is probably backlogged with complaints.

Ogres, Orcs, and Other Monsters

In addition to limited markets and discrimination, sooner or later you are probably going to run into a manager more ogre than human. This kind of character can make even the best job miserable if you don't find some way around the person. The Intolerable Personality can be found anywhere: in insurance companies, banks, or government offices. He or she may be brass and blockheaded or so fearful as to question every move you make until you feel you are back in grade school.

When you run into this character, no matter where, here are some things to keep in mind.

- Is this person going to be around for a long time? If Mr. Obnoxious is close to retirement or transfer, it may be best just to grit your teeth and hang in there rather than plan a campaign that will take longer to set in motion than it's worth.

- Is there a quick way to bypass Mrs. Headache? If she's only a pain to deal with in direct confrontation, can you resort to memorandums and written reports, or channel the work flow through someone close to her?

- Is a specific and temporary problem creating the situation? One woman manager who seemed to delight in creating conflict and wouldn't smile if her life depended on it was actually suffering grief at the loss of a relative; sympathy went a long way to soft-ening her behavior. Often people in positions of power are un-comfortable with themselves; sometimes you can discover what those fears are and provide some nonthreatening feedback and reassurance. But to try these tactics you must be a good reader of personality. If you are not, courses in psychology might help you understand and work around others' personality quirks.

- Is this person reacting to something he sees in you—real or imag-ined? If he is generally obnoxious you know that you are not the issue. If his behavior is heightened by interactions with you, then perhaps a direct confrontation is in order and it is time to request a meeting to try and clear the air. If this is necessary, focus on your feelings ("Yesterday during the meeting I felt your response was unnecessarily abrupt and I wasn't able to give a complete ex-planation of the situation") and not on your interpretation of why this person is behaving so badly. By playing Freud you may only antagonize and threaten.

Attack from the Back—Or from the Side

Problems in the job world don't happen only with those above you. Many women are taken by surprise to find their biggest threat to moving up is from their co-workers, or from those they have left behind. As unfortunate as it may be, we cannot always count on support from the troops—some of whom may be suffering from their own conflicts and taking it out in the safest ways possible. Retaliation is often deflected away from the source of the problem, as in the cartoon of the man who is yelled at by his boss and comes home to scream at his wife, who hollers at her son, who kicks the dog.

Side attacks may come as a shock, especially to feminists who would like to believe that all women are more beautiful than all men, just because they are women. But not all men are the bad guys and not all women wear the white hats. If you are not ready to face this, you may find your best office friend just got that job you applied for, and what's more, she's not even feeling bad about beating you out on the sly. This doesn't mean you should be paranoid and stop supporting others. It just means that most of your energy should be channeled inward, to make sure you get where you are headed.

Child-Care Arrangements

One of the biggest handicaps for women in the workplace is divided attention that comes from worrying about children, or the inability to get into a position in the first place because who will watch Jennifer? Because this issue is vital to all single mothers, a separate chapter is devoted to child-care options.

If you have already successfully worked around the problems that child care can create, you might provide invaluable information to other women you know or meet. This is an area in which all women should be lobbying, at any level, for increased options for women. All too slowly society is accepting a role in providing support for mothers who must work. While many women feel this should be as essential a part of federal budgeting as weapons, many legislators are not sufficiently aware that children really are our greatest resources, entitled to at least as much protection and development as our national parks. Until that happens, we should work to awaken government's and private industry's sense of responsibility for day-care options for working mothers.

Education and Training Experience

Legislation has been enacted to prevent unequal access to training and educational opportunities for women. But women are still bypassed in many training programs that could give them skills for better-paid white-collar and trade vocations. Enrollment of women in most graduate schools has still not reached 50 percent. And women number only a few percent in craft and higher-paid trade occupations.

The situation of women today may be likened to that of black men just after the Civil War. The legislation is there, but it will take several generations for reforms to be enacted. In the meantime, it is up to the individual woman to take advantage of any educational or training program she can discover.

Some of the women interviewed by the Stress and Families Project had been enrolled in government-sponsored training programs (half of which led to new jobs); a few had been able to use welfare as a springboard to college and graduate school; some were developing new skills through programs at their current places of employment (supervisory and management training programs offered in-house). Still others were feeding their needs for personal growth and job enhancement through adult classes and nonacademic workshops.

The opportunities for continuing education are almost endless. According to the National Center for Education Statistics, more than twenty million adults over seventeen participated in continuing educational programs in 1981.[4] These were part-time courses, whether for credit or not.

Colleges and universities accounted for only one fifth of these offerings. One quarter were offered by technical and vocational institutions and community colleges. Another quarter were offered by business and industry, labor unions, and government agencies.

If you are interested in continuing training and education, check with your library to see if your city or town offers a guide similar to that provided by the Educational Exchange of Greater Boston. The Exchange lists courses that provide entry skills in everything from accordion playing and other musical careers to waitress training and washing-machine repair to Zen and zoology.

For additional information on correspondence courses and programs designed specifically for women's advancement, refer to the section "At Least Consider," later in this chapter.

WHERE ARE YOU NOW?

The following three sections are designed to be individually helpful to you depending on your level of work experience. "Starting Out" offers advice for women who need to develop initial working skills; "Moving Up" is aimed at the 80 percent of all working women who find themselves underpaid and/or underutilized in the middle mass of jobs in service and support industries; and "View from the Top" discusses women who plan to make it all the way to the highest positions in their chosen fields. The discussion of networking at the end of this chapter applies to all women—whether one step from the bottom or one step from the top.

STARTING OUT

> How would I define an emotional problem? Well, that means to me something really upsetting and that was me before I got this job. It was really getting me down, sitting in this house. But ever since I got this job, I've been cool, you know?

To be without a job can be frightening and upsetting. It can do an awful number on your self-perception. Many women with young children and little or no paid work experience come to believe they are incapable of being self-sufficient. They come to believe that there is "nothing out there" and resign themselves to a lifetime of scrimping by on welfare checks or inadequate or unreliable child-support and alimony payments. Other women—"displaced homemakers'" or young women without life plans and belief in themselves—often take the first low-paying job they can find and soon settle into jobs that provide little satisfaction and less money.

What separates the woman who feels she has "just the right job" from the woman who hates leaving the house in the morning or settles uneasily into inadequate support? Knowing what you want and feeling confident about performing your special skills to the best of your ability are two essential ingredients to success as a working woman.

Obviously, some women have the jump on others when it comes to knowing what to look for and feeling less hesitant about their ability to perform well. Some of the things that can help are:

- Parental support and encouragement
- The amount of education and training provided early in life
- Guidance from others who have the information we need
- Strong personal incentives for doing well

The expectation that we can and should be seeking well-paid and satisfying jobs is perhaps the most important factor. And this expectation is one that too few women have grown up with, or are currently making a part of their lives, even though most women today do end up working.

All but a few of the 243 women interviewed by the Stress and Families Project had held jobs in their lifetimes. Somehow most women overcome numerous barriers to employment (lack of education and experience, lack of knowledge about what is available and how to get it, limited child-care and transportation problems). Whether you are a twenty-year-old woman with small children or a fifty-year-old displaced homemaker, it may be helpful to remember that another woman in another place has been in your shoes. If you haven't worked, or have very limited paid work experience, the chances are that you have some misconceptions about yourself and about working.

The misconceptions about yourself probably include fears that you have no marketable skills. Misconceptions about the workplace probably include the idea that you are qualified to pursue only one or two kinds of jobs. But if you need to work, which seems apparent if you are a single mother, you are going to have to overcome these misconceptions simultaneously: getting a better idea of who you are and all you have to offer, while finding out just what is available to you.

You may actually have little difficulty adjusting to a job and performing well in it, but how do you find one that suits your needs in the first place? Can you wade through the confusion by yourself, or should you seek help in your job search? For many women the most successful path to entry into the workplace has come from a combination of these approaches; after doing some homework on their own, they were able to contact others who could provide the information they needed for landing them in their first jobs.

Personal Assessment: Who Am I?

If you are unfamiliar with what you want to do and have to offer it is time to clarify these basics. If you have been channeling most of your time and energy into a man or into your children (or both) you may face the universal women's dilemma: Who am *I?* When it comes time to sell your skills, what do you want to offer the marketplace and how can you get the most money for the exchange?

If you have picked a career path and are pretty sure it is the one you want to follow, you might want to skip ahead to "The Importance of Appearance." If you haven't a clue about the type of job that may appeal to you, don't despair; within two weeks you should have a list of ten types of jobs in your hand and be preparing yourself for your first round of interviews.

This is going to take some preparation on your part, but two weeks is not a lot of time to spend preparing for a lifetime of working experience. Since it's up to you to make the upcoming years as rewarding as they can possibly be, the initial steps you take make the difference between underpaid and well paid.

To start, pick a time when you have a half hour or so free and jot down on paper the ten things that you have done best in your life—things you do well and enjoy doing.

These could include anything from preparing gourmet meals to fixing broken toys and appliances, driving a car, telling stories to your child, playing volleyball, bowling, dancing, writing essays, helping plan your church socials, or keeping the records for your women's club.

Next to each activity, list the skills you use in carrying them out. For example, fixing broken appliances takes concentration, patience, deductive logic for problem solving, skill with tools, and so forth. Storytelling requires an active imagination, verbal and other communication skills, and a relaxed approach to contact with others. Driving a car well requires alertness, quick reflexes, hand-eye coordination, and the ability to make rapid judgments. Take your time and be thorough.

Once you have your list of ten strengths, make a list of the ten things you most *dis*like doing and/or that you feel you do very badly. Be as honest about your weaknesses as about your strengths. If you hate cooking and would just as soon have TV dinners or take-home chicken each night, if you hate to iron, if you have no use for mechanical appliances of any kind, put these down. We can't do everything well. All of us do some things poorly and some things better than average. The point is to be honest and analyze yourself objectively.

Taking a look at your strong points and your weak ones will give you an idea of your own personal patterns. Do you prefer working with others or are you more of an introvert? Do the things you enjoy involve data (written communication), people, or things? How do you express yourself best? Maybe you are very shy with strangers but find yourself a genius at the sewing machine. Maybe you hate being cooped up in the house but find real zest in outdoor activities such as trimming hedges. Do you prefer active endeavors (on your feet and moving) or are you a sitter? Do you find yourself being most creative with children, or men or women, or older persons? Are you comfortable in crowds and do you love selling things or ideas, or would you be just as happy to keep your two best friends and no others for the rest of your life?

Your preferences should give you ideas about where to begin looking, and where *not* to look. For example, even if it is a fast-growing, relatively well-paid field, there is no point in trying to remold yourself for a career in computer programming if you hate figures and flunked algebra. To be successful in anything, you have to be able to use your best skills.

Next, armed with your list, visit your library, your greatest community resource. There you should find at least one of the three books discussed below. These will supply you with the next bit of information you need—specific kinds of jobs you can apply for. After you locate these jobs, you will find out if these jobs are available in your community at a reasonable commuting distance, and what their long-range forecast is—whether or not the field you choose is "endangered" (by becoming obsolete or computerized).

The Dictionary of Occupational Titles (*DOT*) has been put together by the U.S. Department of Labor's Employment and Training Administration to answer the needs of the public-employment-service system. Though the DOT is used by state employment agencies to match people to jobs available, you can use it also to find any one of over twenty thousand jobs currently available in the United States. If you think that as a woman you are limited to teaching, waitressing, or sales, the DOT will soon broaden your horizons.

The DOT lists jobs in three ways:

(1) Occupational Group Arrangement lists jobs by code numbers indicating the type of work, training required, physical demand, and working conditions.

(2) Alphabetical Index of Occupational Titles lists job titles only.

(3) Occupational Titles arranged by industry. This is helpful if you know the industry you would like to work in and want to know the variety of jobs available within that industry.

The Occupational Group Arrangement of jobs is probably where you should begin. Each occupation has a "Lead Statement" that summarizes the job and tells what a worker does; the purpose of the work; whether tools, equipment, machinery, or other work aids are required; the products made; and so on. The "Task Element Statements," which follow the Lead, indicate specific tasks the worker performs in the job.

Use the DOT (ask your librarian for help if you need it) to find ten interesting jobs that you are qualified to do, or could become qualified for with minimal training. The DOT is an extensive handbook, so you may want to spend a few afternoons going through it. What you will be doing is matching your experience (don't forget volunteer work) against the requirements of ten jobs that sound interesting to you, and are not too exotic. If you need further information you might want to check out another valuable and excellent reference source.

The Encyclopedia of Careers and Vocational Guidance, published by Doubleday, is designed primarily for people starting out in jobs or choosing careers and offers a wealth of information in two volumes. Volume I aids in planning your career. It provides useful and easy-to-read articles on how to understand yourself, how to discover and evaluate your interests, aptitudes, and abilities, and how to make the best use of the results of guidance and personality tests. It also provides you with information on schooling, how and where to borrow money for tuition, and how the world of work is changing.

Volume II will give you specific information about the career you want to explore. If your only work experience has been waitressing, you might check the Encyclopedia entry about the Food Industry to discover it is a high-growth business which has gone from $46-billion-a-year in 1960 to about $200 billion in the mid-1970s. You could also look up alternative careers and learn what it would take for you to become a quality-control worker in the food-processing industry.

While embarking on your job search, bear in mind that deciding about jobs is a continuing process. You may not now be qualified for the job of your dreams, but reference sources and placement or counseling services can provide you with information about steppingstone jobs that can move you up the ladder.

The Occupational Outlook Handbook is published by the U.S. Department of Labor. Once you have your list of ten job possibilities, refer to the OOH. There you will find—in addition to more than five hundred job descriptions and information on requirements and working conditions—the more important facts on possible earnings and future employment trends. This information is especially useful to prevent wrong-path decisions. It will do you little good, for example, to channel money and energy into pursuing a career in widget-making if in ten years the call for widgets is going to be zero. Since the OOH predicts future opportunities, you might find a field where you can get in on the ground floor and work up.

Allow yourself a good week to become acquainted with (1) jobs of interest to you that match your skills and preferences (2) in fields that have good growth possibilities. If you need help in doing this, consider other input from:

- State employment agencies;
- Private counselors;
- High-school or college guidance centers which may provide aptitude testing and other skills-matching information;
- Friends, who may be more objective about your potential, especially those friends you consider successful in their work endeavors.

Your next steps will be putting together the rest of your personal packaging.

The Problem with Résumés

The problem with résumés is that everyone needs one (they are now as necessary for a working person as a driver's license is for most adults), and one that looks good can get you farther than one that looks bad.

All résumés are expected to look neat, be well typed, and be designed to show your credentials for a particular job as succinctly as possible. But employers also look for résumés that show a steady rise in responsibility and raises and that indicate a reasonably long time at each job—so that an employer can gauge the likelihood you will be around long enough for his investment in your training to pay off for him.

Many women have résumés that some employers believe indicate "poor risks"—an intermittent job history with time out for childbirth and/or child rearing. Unfortunately, in the United States you may be penalized for any interludes in your investment in a particular job. (In Sweden, the government has a much more progressive attitude toward work and families.)

While some headway is being made to humanize the work-place by incorporating child-care options and flextime work schedules for mothers, progress is slow. Someday employers may place a higher value on the experience you have gained as a mother. For now, do not be apologetic, but realize this atti-tude is something you will have to work around.

Do not feel discouraged if your paid-job history is scanty. You can and should bolster your résumé with school activities, club activities, and volunteer work in which you have learned valuable skills and acquired experience in working with others.

A wealth of information about résumé preparation is avail-able at your library, and some books provide samples. Because résumés are often a foot in the door of a prospective employer, if you can afford it, you should seek out some professional help in putting yours together. Again, a friend may be invaluable. Help may also be found at women's centers, displaced-home-makers centers, or seminars in job searching. If you need addi-tional help in personnel guidance and counseling, write the American Personnel and Guidance Association, Two Skyline Plaza, Suite 400, 5203 Leesburg Pike, Falls Church, Virginia 22041. Its Directory of Counseling Agencies lists places where good counseling service is available.

Explore the Market

Even in times of economic recession, jobs are available. But how do we find them? Some of the major sources of job infor-mation come from the following places:

- Word of mouth. Friends and relatives are handy for letting you know of openings they hear about. Make it known that you are looking, and ask friends to pass the word along. Many women have made connections from "the old girls network," which grows larger every day.

- Local, state, and federal employment agencies. In addition to let-ting you know what is available in your area, these offices provide services like free counseling.

Also check with your state Occupational Information Coordinating Committee, a recently established agency, to help you find career information tailored to your situation. A list of titles and addresses for offices in each state is available from the *Occupational Outlook Handbook* and is reprinted under the "More Information" section of the *Encyclopedia of Careers and Vocational Guidance.*

- Check into civil service jobs that may be available. They require that you pass one or more tests and an oral evaluation interview, but any government agency is apt to be more active in complying with affirmative-action guidelines to seek qualified women applicants. For more information on Civil Service jobs, write: Office of Personnel Management, 1800 E Street, Washington, D.C. 20415
- Chamber of Commerce. Your local chamber lists manufacturers and other employers in your area. If you are aware of a specific industry you'd like to be working with, this may be a good bet for places to send your résumé.
- High-school and college career-planning and placement offices.
- Classified advertisements in national, local, underground and women's newspapers.
- Personnel offices of larger employers: hospitals, universities, or private businesses. Don't be afraid to walk in and ask about jobs, which may be prominently posted or listed with a personnel placement worker.
- Private employment agencies. Call several and find out if they specialize in the kinds of jobs you are interested in.
- Religious organizations.
- Women's centers.
- Classifications in trade journals.

The Importance of Appearance

Uncomfortable as they may be, interviews are a necessary part of the job search, and how you appear can often mean success or failure in an interview. This doesn't mean you have to go out shopping for a dress-for-success suit. But it does mean that you give thought to what you wear and how you can present a total image. Even if you are quaking inside—in fact especially then—it is important that you look like you are all together. Be sure to:

- Allow yourself enough time for preparation and prompt arrival, especially if you don't know where the interview is being held.

- Plan to wear a dress you are comfortable in; err on the conservative rather than the flamboyant side.

- Allow yourself a good hour to go over the body basics of clean hair and nails and add a little extra deodorant to balance out the tensions that interviewing can create.

- Have a pen and small notebook handy in your uncluttered purse. Note in advance any questions you have about fringe benefits (which shows an employer you are interested in long-range employment), pay-scale probabilities, job hours, and the like. Referring to notes makes you look more efficient and businesslike than stammering and forgetting what you wanted to ask.

- Remember to make eye contact as quickly as possible and to smile. If a handshake seems appropriate, make it a firm one.

- Speak clearly and firmly and be prepared with all the necessary facts, like the hours you can and can't work, how you feel about weekend or evening overtime, and what your long-range goals are.

- Be aware of the questions that you do not have to answer—that are, in fact, illegal for an employer to ask—such as your age, your birth-control methods, your child-care arrangements, your marital status and religious beliefs.

- Get all essential information (and jot it down in your notebook if necessary). What are the *specific* duties, is there a training period, for whom would you be working, can you see a job description?

- Be confident. Imagine *you* are sitting behind the desk—would you feel more comfortable hiring someone who let you know she could perform the job well, or someone who hemmed and hawed about her abilities?

- Be prepared to talk about yourself and what your strengths are, but listen carefully for potential mismatches between what you want and what the job has to offer.

Although you are being interviewed, you should be prepared to interview back. It may put you more at ease to remember that the interview is a two-way process. You may not be suited to every job you interview for, and just as you may be turned down for one you want, you should be prepared to turn down one that you discover is not really for you. Be as active at finding out what your prospective job has to offer as you are at selling yourself and making it clear that you are the most outstanding and dynamic woman applying for the job.

A job interview is not the time to be humble and self-effacing. If you need practice brushing up on your confidence and projecting your feelings of competence, you may want to do a few practice interviews for jobs you are pretty sure you don't want, or do a trial run with a friend who can play employer for you.

You've Landed It: What Do You Do with It?

Each job you hold will offer possibilities and drawbacks; no job is perfect. But what your first one or two jobs afford you is the opportunity to establish a record of performance. For at least six months, be prompt and don't leave early. Take your responsibilities seriously. If you have free time, look for opportunities to learn other facets of your job or demonstrate that you are capable of expanding your horizons. If, for instance, you have gotten into a sales position and you have had no customers for twenty minutes, check your inventory, get to know your products, think about ways to display goods more attractively—without making a big deal of it—and make sure your supervisor knows what you are doing.

Think Big and Think UP

Learn what is required of those on the next rung up. If you feel you have supervisory potential, for instance, find out the job requirements of a floor supervisor or office manager. Remember to view your job as just one steppingstone, not a permanent niche within the organization. Even with a built-in inflationary annual increase, the fastest way to improve your life-style is to find a job with a higher salary. This job will come with increased responsibilities, and only if you are looking, and are ready to assume those responsibilities, will you be in line for a move up.

MOVING UP

OK. You've made it into the workplace and you have worked your way up from that first terrified anxiety. You've learned a lot: You know you can survive, you can be dependable despite the pressure of mothering and marketing yourself simultaneously, and you can be creative. Your juggling act has gotten more and more smooth.

But about this time, what's happening? You are probably finding out that you can do a lot more than you ever thought you could. And you are probably feeling it is time to move on—up in the organization or out into a new field which may hold more interest for you. You are probably facing one or more concerns at this time:

- You like the job but find inflation is eating your check faster than your annual raises are adding to it.
- You may find that the job has become deadly dull and you're losing interest in going in each day; there may be a job in the company that you'd like to shoot for but you think it's beyond your capabilities right now.
- You are feeling eager to explore new territory, with another organization that can teach you new skills.

Most people go through periodic changes in their work life. Having mastered a set of skills, it is not unusual for a person to grow faster than the job permits. Staying with a job which greatly underutilizes your potential can be deadly. Once you can handle the work standing on your head, it's time to think of moving on—to something more challenging and more profitable—either within your present company, at another company, or in a new field. If possible, you should be thinking of ways to move on before the job becomes boring or totally unsatisfactory.

It is time to move on if you are sure that:

- You have learned all the important skills the job had to teach you;
- You have made as many potentially helpful contacts as you possibly can there;
- You have taken advantage of any and all educational side benefits the job may offer (training programs; tuition or conference benefits that you could make immediate use of).

If you decide to stick with your present employer but there is no position available to move up and into at this point, is it possible to have your job upgraded and your title changed?

Is the Company Keeping Up with You?

Some women have been able to create new jobs out of old ones by learning and applying new skills and by taking on more responsibility. It is a short jump, for instance, from secretary to administrative assistant. But the salary and title that come with the latter are going to look a lot more impressive on a résumé.

It is likely you have been doing some amount of this job upgrading. But you probably haven't been taking full credit for it by requesting additional salary increases or by officially rewriting your job description. Even if you are planning on having a new job in two months, every bit of upgrading helps. The more money you are making in a job, the more you can request from your next position. And the more responsible a position you have, the more interesting and responsible job you can shoot for tomorrow.

Periodically make notes (once a month is a good idea)—in one specific work-related notebook—about position changes you create or inherit. If you design a new filing system or new company forms, if you take over supervisory functions for part-time or summer help, make notes of what you did and when. Often your boss will not be aware of all the innovations you make in your position or the increasing responsibilities you assume. And if you are keeping up a fast pace you may soon forget that the job you end up handling is much more complicated than the one you started out with.

These notes will help you build a case, to be presented at the proper moment, for a salary increase or job reevaluation. Some companies are notorious for heaping on a heavier and heavier load for no increased return. It is your responsibility to see you don't end up as an underpaid and overloaded burro. If you have the facts and figures when it comes time for your next evaluation, this is less likely to happen.

Up or Out?

If you can't turn your present job into one with more money and a more impressive title, you can either examine all potential avenues within your organization (don't forget branch offices, if any) or begin to cast nets into related or altogether new career paths.

Try to avoid some of these pitfalls:

- Think "active." You have to make your own breaks. If you don't, you could end up like Good Old Sally, the woman hidden away in accounting who has been in the same room longer than the light fixtures.

- Remember that your job is just a stepping-stone. You are there to learn and to establish a record of competence. But as you master your job you must be looking for a way to use what you've learned to move a little higher.

- Plan to leave each job before you get to the end of your rope. It is easier to find a new job while you have one—but if you wait too long, until things get unbearable or your energy is totally sapped, you may end up taking a job that is less than you wanted, just for a change.

- Each new job should offer you more money and more challenge. There is nothing to recommend a lateral change. Moving hori-

zontally is just a waste of time unless your present job is so unbearable that it is doing a number on your mental health.

• If you must tread water until a better job comes along, reexplore
any perks that you haven't yet taken advantage of (for example,
in-house training programs or tuition reimbursements for job-re-
lated course work, group-dynamics seminars or sessions in computer orientation).

• Don't allow yourself to get so overloaded that you can't see what
else may be available around you. A better job may pass you by
while you've got your head buried under someone else's overflow.

At Least Consider

Perhaps, for one reason or another, you simply cannot stand
the thought of being back in a classroom. But unless you are
sure that you have all the education you are going to need for
the next twenty or thirty years, you should at least consider
additional educational or training courses at some point. As
more highly educated young women enter the work force each
year, it will become increasingly difficult for bright but less
educated women to move into well-paid jobs. The world is
moving toward more specialization and no one who works can
afford to stop learning.

If you haven't finished your high-school—or college—training, you should, of course, do so as soon as possible. You won't
be the only adult in your classes, because more women each
year are returning to school to do exactly what you may need
to do—increase their marketability.

If you have no time or money to put into college or university training right now, plan to pick up at least some college
credits, perhaps through evening classes or on weekends. You
may be able to gain credits—and confidence—through "life-
experience credits." These are college credits obtained without
course work, in areas in which you have gained knowledge
through life experience. Such experience can be translated into
college credits by taking a College Level Examination Program
(CLEP) test.

More than twelve hundred colleges and universities offer CLEP examinations,[5] which, if you pass them, mean instant college credit on your résumé. For more information, contact your local college or university or write to: CLEP, College Entrance Examination Board, P.O. B. 592, Princeton, New Jersey 08540.

Alternative educational opportunities include the following:

The *University Without Walls* offers no prescribed curriculum or set time for completion of degrees. Programs are individually designed for each student's needs. Information can be obtained from Union for Experimenting Colleges and Universities, Antioch College, Yellow Springs, Ohio 45387.

The Women's Bureau of the U.S. Department of Labor reports that almost all states sponsor special educational programs for women over thirty-five. For a copy of *Continuing Education Programs and Services for Women,* write to The Women's Bureau, Department of Labor, 200 Constitution Avenue N.W., Washington, D.C. 20210, or Superintendent of Documents, U.S. Government Printing Office, Washington, D.C. 20402.

Lucia Bequaert (*Single Women: Alone and Together*) suggests two other sources of information which may prove valuable. For information on correspondence courses that offer college credit, write to The National University Extension Association, University of Minnesota, Room 112, Building TSMC, Minneapolis, Minnesota 55455. Or you might want to write to the following organization to see if there is a local chapter near you: AWARE (The Association for Women's Active Return to Education), 5810 Wilshire Boulevard, Suite 605, Los Angeles, California 90036.

Final Reminders

Whether you have just moved into a new and more challenging position or are beginning to think of moving up or out, certain do's and don'ts from *The Ambitious Woman's Guide to a Successful Career* will give you the best chance of getting the recognition and raises you deserve.

- Observe what goes on around you, not just the work that hits your desk. To expand your skills and increase your paycheck, keep abreast of as much of your organization as possible; know who's in power and who isn't. Keep an eye on bulletin boards, memos sent to your boss, and all available company communiqués and newsletters.

- Find ways to increase your visibility. If the big boss has an opening for a capable manager, she won't think of you if she doesn't even know you are there. Women often find it difficult to be in the spotlight or call attention to special accomplishments. As part of your self-promotion, let your boss know how well you handled a crusty client or worked overtime to come up with a cost-effective solution. If you have a clear, well-thought-out proposal, don't be afraid to submit it—before someone else does. If you attend meetings or conferences for your boss, make sure that others know your name.

- Set definite goals and periodically assess your progress in reaching them.

- Project your feelings of confidence. If you need—or soon will need—a new area of expertise, learn what you need to know, even if that means taking a night course in accounting or taking reports home several weekends in a row.

- Know your organizational chart. Inadvertently offending a vice president is the kind of lasting impression you don't want to make.

- Don't gossip. Gossip and negative remarks have a way of circulating through the grapevine with amazing speed, picking up distortions along the way. You need a reputation as a trustworthy employee—one who can keep secrets if she needs to.

- Don't let your relationship with your boss slip. Find as many ways as possible to make the relationship mutually beneficial. Your boss must see you as a capable person in your own right. The more indispensable you become, the more you are going to be rewarded. Higginson and Quick suggest four ways you can make that happen:

Talk to people s/he doesn't want to talk to. A tactful approach might be, "Since you are so tied up with budget proposals, would you like me to call Mr. Burnside?"

Get information your boss can't. Whether your boss is too busy, handicapped by her position, or simply unwilling to appear anxious for certain information, you may be faster at getting information she needs for some particular venture.

Provide skills your boss lacks. No one has it all. And since you and your boss are a team, it is natural that you will be more expert at some things and able to fill in gaps at appropriate moments. There will be times when *your* ideas will make *him* look good, but as long as this is not an everyday occurrence and he shows his appreciation at appraisal time, this kind of exchange is expected.

Cover for him. This last issue can be tricky: It doesn't mean you help your boss out in some illegal activity, but it may mean bending the truth upon occasion. (Your boss may take a three-hour lunch to deal with a marital problem the afternoon the home office VP calls up looking for him.) You will have to develop your own rule of thumb for how far out on a limb you will go, but you might want to consider:

Whether your assistance might boomerang if your boss later resents your involvement in his "weakness/wrongdoing."
Whether you will suffer if your boss gets caught.
How extensively and how often it might cause you to lie.
Whether your boss's actions are hurting the organization.

In the final analysis, your level of drive and your belief in yourself will mean the difference between success or second place, between finding satisfying jobs in your career or staying with those that make you hate getting up in the morning.

A certain amount of risk taking is involved each time a woman moves up the ladder. Some women cannot deal with the anxieties of change and challenge; it is tempting to take the safe road. But the more successful women you meet—and this is one very important reason to get into a network where you can meet other successful women—the faster your anxieties will be relieved. There is nothing like a bit of advice from someone who has been there—and has come out on top.

VIEW FROM THE TOP

Money, power, prestige—these are some of the things you will find in a position at the top. While only an exceptional man reaches the heights in any field, with today's inequalities only a *very* exceptional *woman* reaches those heights.

Most women working their way up corporate, craft, or academic ladders are still feeling the pressures of being female groundbreakers, and some still worry that they succeeded only because they were "token women." But most women, like most men, arrive at the top because they exhibit special talents, drive, and unlimited capacity for work.

The view from the top has mixed blessings; you pay a price for the ride up. What does it take to get there? Margaret Hennig, associate professor at Simmons College and co-author of *The Managerial Woman,* studied a group of top-level (presidents and vice-presidents) women executives to see what they had in common. While her findings are not infallible signposts of what you need to assure yourself a five- or six-digit annual income, her work does indicate that the woman at the top doesn't usually get there by luck alone. These are some of the common denominators among the group of women Hennig investigated:

- Each woman was either the first-born or the only child in her family. (As has been demonstrated by other studies, parents are prone to encourage only or first-born children to greater heights of achievement.)

- Each had been encouraged to explore nontraditional roles (that is, there was little if any pushing to "learn to type" or "get yourself a good, steady secretarial job").

- Each had unusually close relationships with her father—something that immediately separates these women from millions of others who were raised to feel apologetic for not having been sons.

- Each was allowed or encouraged to participate, if she wished, in "boy's activities" as a child.

- Not surprisingly, each woman displayed an advanced sense of her own self-esteem.

What these factors add up to is a childhood and young adulthood free from the standard mythologies of "the natural woman" as one who is passive, intellectually handicapped, and nonassertive.

These findings closely parallel those that emerged at the New York Academy of Sciences Conferences in 1972 and resulted in the book *Women and Success: The Anatomy of Achievement.* In that book, the importance of a father's encouragement was discussed by Marjorie Lozoff of the Wright Institute at Berkeley:

> When the fathers of young women . . . treated their daughters as if they were interesting people worthy and deserving of respect and encouragement, these fathers imparted to the women that their femininity was not endangered by the development of talent, that the fathers did not feel threatened by a female pushing forward with ambition. When they encouraged development of talent, one could say that the fathers gave their daughters 'permission to be whole persons, to develop a variety of interests without concern that their femininity was at stake.'

But maternal role modeling can also be a very positive influence in developing aspirations in young women. Lozoff says, "On the other hand, when women have career-oriented mothers, the daughters tend to develop a variety of talents and interests at an early age."

In short, success often breeds success. Though some women at the top make it with very little encouragement, a supportive environment will increase your odds. And it is not just early family influence that can make the difference. One of the most helpful things is to find supportive successful women who are actively networking to help other women (and themselves) in the same ways that men have done by using "old boy networks."

But Hennig found two other essentials, common among the corporate executives in her study:

Mentors. Each executive managed to connect with a male manager who was several steps up in the organization. These men provided encouragement and mentoring for their protégées, enabling the women to move higher. This is not to say that all mentors are men. In the field of publishing, for example, there are many women at the top. And more women are working up from the ranks in many occupations. (With men or women, mentoring is a policy that can work well on any level, not just in the upper stratosphere.)

Specialization. Each woman came to conceive of herself as a specialist. She concentrated her energy on becoming an expert in her technical area.

No Free Lunch

What is seldom stressed by superachiever women is the price you pay for channeling most of your energy into work achievement. If your career is the most important thing in the world to you, you may not see the loss of other goals as a sacrifice. What was sacrificed by the women Hennig studied was an extensive family life. Half of the women married older men who are also considered superachievers. Most felt their relationships were satisfying but "togetherness time" was minimal.

It is apparent that no one can have it all. Few institutions encourage dual roles in their employees. With an $80,000-plus salary, most companies feel justified in asking for a near 100 percent commitment. Too many afternoons off for taking the kids to the dentist are the frowned-upon exception rather than the rule. In the long run, you had better be prepared to see your company as your second, and sometimes primary, family.

That is a commitmment few women are fully prepared to make. But if you are prepared for such a commitment, there is no reason why you should stop short now. Keep going over those reports and keep the following personal characteristics in mind.

Willpower. Being continually in the spotlight requires not only that you look the part but that you feel the part. Often you will get things accomplished by sheer will and force of personality. Having a clear image of yourself as a dynamic, capable woman is essential.

High self-esteem. Whenever and wherever, find ways to bolster your confidence level. If you are aware of an area of weakness, one which might cause problems for you down the road, plan some self-education time to fill the gap.

Competitiveness. This is not a dirty word; it is an essential part of your performance.

High energy level. Get the sleep you need to carry you through. The slot you are shooting for isn't a nine-to-five one; it's going to take all you've got to give.

Ambition. See that next step up and hold that image in your mind until you've got the title to go with it. Then don't forget to look ahead to where you will go from there.

Candor. Some top managers play it close to the vest, but Hennig found that successful women were candid with themselves and with others. This doesn't mean giving your hand away, but don't beat around the bush or come across as indecisive.

Risk taking. If you tremble on the brink as others leap across the murky waters, you just may find yourself out of the race. Unless you take risks, you will never know how far you could have gone. To win you sometimes have to gamble; there are no two ways about it. What can increase your odds, however, is plugging into the best network you can find.

NETWORKING

Networking, a concept of trading resources with others, is not a new idea. Women have been networking for centuries, trading healing recipes, personal experiences, and encouragement, or helping each other out in time of childbirth and family death. But women haven't—as men always have—been networking for purposes of increasing their options in the paid work force.

A network is a concentrated information bank that can save

you time (once you have invested a little into it), money, and needless feelings of isolation in your work life. A network is a group of women who are interested in thriving business lives and are willing to share what they know. Such women have created active networks all over the country—in advertising, construction, law, architecture, insurance, medicine, banking, the arts, the media, and a hundred other markets. They have gathered together to share their experiences and knowledge as filmmakers, fashion designers, musicians, nurses and doctors, politicians, ministers, labor unionists, journalists, carpenters, certified public accountants, typists and secretaries, composers, and farm workers. (There are, of course, mixed-sex networks and networks composed solely of men. This discussion focuses on women's networks, but you may find some mixed networks equally helpful.)

You may need a small, relatively specialized network like the Washington Forum, a women's group in the capital. Or you might benefit most right now from the support of a large and fast-growing "grassroots" organization like "9 to 5," Women Office Workers of Boston. Whatever kind of network you need, finding the right one can change your life as it has for millions of other women, once you begin to firm up your ideas of what you want and have done a little homework about you and the state of work.

Women's networks function for a variety of purposes:[7]

- To share information about available career opportunities;
- To serve as support systems for working women;
- To gather successful women together who can serve as role models for other businesswomen;
- To offer skills training;
- To expose women to a broader variety of world experience and opinion;
- To increase the visibility of women leaders in the community.

In short, networking offers women increased opportunities for professional development.

Whatever field you are now in probably has at least one active group of women who meet together periodically to exchange information. In some fields, women all across the country get together in small groups once a month or more to share what they have discovered about the particular problems and joys in their professional lives.

Some networks are mainly interested in the basic issues of equal pay for equal work, increased private-industry support for child-care facilities, or eliminating promotional discrimination against women. Other groups meet for specialized reasons, such as promoting women business owners in their community. Women's networks vary in their influence, an influence greatly increased through numbers.

Effective networks do not fall into your lap—they are lines and circles you help create and strengthen as you develop and use your growing talents. In return for sharing your work-related experiences and knowledge, you can receive the benefits of expertise and support from other women who share your goals and energy.

If you haven't already plugged into an active, productive network, or if you are thinking of developing a more specialized network than the one(s) you are now in, Mary Scott Welch's *NETWORKING* can provide you with information on how to get started.

Source Notes
1. Mary Scott Welch, *NETWORKING* (New York: Warner Books, 1980).
2. Matina Horner and Mary Walsh, "Psychological Barriers to Success in Women," *Women and Success: The Anatomy of Achievement,* ed. Ruth Kundsin (New York: William Morrow, 1974).
3. Marjorie Lozoff, "Fathers and Autonomy in Women," *Women and Success,* p. 105.
4. Educational Exchange of Greater Boston.
5. Margaret Higginson, and Thomas Quick, *The Ambitious Woman's Guide to a Successful Career,* A Division of the American Management Association (AMACOM), 1975.

6. Lozoff, loc. cit.
7. Welch, op. cit.

References

Bailyn, Lotte. "Family Constraints on Women's Work." *Women and Success: The Anatomy of Achievement,* ed. Ruth Kundsin. New York: William Morrow, 1974.

Bergmann, Barbara. "The Economics of Women's Liberation." *Women and Success: The Anatomy of Achievement,* ed. Ruth Kundsin. New York: William Morrow, 1974.

Bequaert, Lucia. *Single Women: Alone and Together.* Boston: Beacon Press, 1976.

Curtis, Jean. *A Guide for Working Mothers.* New York: Simon & Schuster, 1976.

Hennig, Margaret. "Family Dynamics and the Successful Woman Executive," *Women and Success,* ed. Ruth Kundsin. New York: William Morrow, 1974.

Higginson, Margaret, and Thomas Quick. *The Ambitious Woman's Guide to a Successful Career.* AMACOM, 1975.

Horner, Matina, and Mary Walsh. "Psychological Barriers to Success in Women," *Women and Success,* ed. Ruth Kundsin. New York: William Morrow, 1974.

Lozoff, Marjorie. "Fathers and Autonomy in Women," *Women and Success,* ed. Ruth Kundsin. New York: William Morrow, 1974.

Murdock, Carol. *Single Parents Are People Too.* New York: Butterick, 1980.

Schlayer, Mary Elizabeth, and Marilyn Cooley. *How to Be a Financially Secure Woman.* New York: Rawson, 1978.

Tebbets, Ruth. "Work: Its Meaning for Women's Lives," *Lives in Stress: Women and Depression,* ed. D. Belle. Beverly Hills, Calif.: Sage, 1982.

Welch, Mary Scott. *NETWORKING.* * New York: Warner Books, 1980.

* Highly recommended.

Index